THE COMPLETE 2022 EDITION
MEDITERRANEAN
Diet Cookbook
– FOR BEGINNERS –

Nancy Santini

TABLE OF CONTENTS

Story of the Mediterranean Diet

The Mediterranean diet is a dietary regime, typical of countries in the Mediterranean area, that many studies have linked to countless health benefits, especially in the prevention of cancer, cardiovascular and neurodegenerative diseases, and in 2010 it has been declared by UNESCO an Intangible Heritage of Humanity. It is a lifestyle that is more than a simple way of eating, more of an eating pattern but, rather, a set of knowledge, social practices, and cultural traditions that have been historically passed down by people living in the Mediterranean. since the post-war period.

How the Mediterranean Diet was born?

The first observational study that led to the explanation of the concept of the "Mediterranean diet" and to understand its benefits, which became popular as the "study of seven countries", was conducted by American biologist and physiologist Ancel Keys in the 1940s.

Keys, who was in Crete during the period following allied troops, said the incidence of cardiovascular disease on the island was lower than in the United States. A few years later, in 1944, in Paestum, he made the same observation about the population of Cilento and predicted that the low incidence of heart disease might be related to diet.

He moved to the village of Cilento, Pioppi, where he observed more the diet of the local people: he noticed farmers in villages of Southern Italy who were low on fat diets of animal origin and above all was made of bread and pasta or soup., often eaten with legumes, seasonal fruits, and vegetables from their gardens, extra virgin olive oil, cheese, dried fruit, and wine. These practices, both for the farmers of Cilento and the inhabitants of the island of Crete, resulted in higher longevity and lower incidence of cardiovascular diseases than those observed in the citizens of Northern Europe and the United States. of America.

Benefits of the Mediterranean Diet

Many scientific pieces of research have shown that the Mediterranean diet plays an important role in the prevention of cardiovascular diseases and other pathologies such as cancer, obesity, diabetes, osteoporosis, and mental problems. . The beneficial effects of this diet are associated with many factors, such as the richness of low-calorie foods (vegetables, fruits, cereals, and legumes), which help to maintain a healthy weight and ensure the use of fiber that protects from scratch. of many chronic diseases. The Mediterranean diet is also characterized by low-fat content, mostly unsaturated, and by high intake of antioxidants,

Most studies done on the Mediterranean diet have shown its effectiveness in maintaining good overall health. Extensively demonstrated how the Mediterranean diet reduces the incidence of:

A. Bowel cancer
B. Breast neoplasia
C. Diabetes
D. Infarction

E. Atherosclerosis
F. Hypertension
G. Digestive diseases
H. Prevents metabolic syndrome - which is one of the main causes of the emergence of cardiovascular diseases.

Clean Fifteen and Dirty Dozen Lists for 2022

Here's the Environmental Working Group's annual guide, which includes Dirty Dozen and Clean lists of non-organic fruits with the most and least pesticides:

Dirty Dozen
- Strawberries
- Spinach
- Kale, cabbage, and mustard greens
- nectarines
- Apples
- Grapes
- Bell and hot peppers
- Cherries
- Peaches
- Pears
- Celery
- Tomatoes

Clean Fifteen
- Avocados
- Sweet corn
- Pineapple
- Onions
- Papaya
- Frozen Peas
- asparagus
- Honeydew melon
- Kiwi
- Cabbage
- Mushrooms
- Cantaloupe
- Mangoes
- Watermelon
- Sweet potatoes

Cooking Conversion Chart

Teaspoon and Tablespoon Measures

Dash or pinch	=	less than 1/8 teaspoon
1 1/2 teaspoons	=	1/2 tablespoon
3 teaspoons	=	1 tablespoon; 1/2 fluid ounce
4 1/2 teaspoons	=	1 1/2 tablepsoons
2 tablespoons	=	1/8 cup; 1 fluid ounce
4 tablespoons	=	1/4 cup; 2 fluid ounces
8 tablespoons	=	1/2 cup; 4 fluid ounces
12 tablespoons	=	3/4 cup; 6 fluid ounces
16 tablespoons	=	1 cup; 8 fluid ounces; 1/2 pint

Cup Measures

1/8 cup	=	2 tablespoons; 1 fluid ounce
1/4 cup	=	4 tablespoons; 2 fluid ounces
1/3 cup	=	5 tablespoons plus 1 teaspoon
1/2 cup	=	8 tablespoons; 4 fluid ounces
2/3 cup	=	10 tablespoons plus 2 teaspoons
3/4 cup	=	12 tablespoons; 6 fluid ounces
7/8 cup	=	3/4 cup plus 2 tablespoons
1 cup	=	16 tablespoons; 8 fluid ounces; 1/2 pint
2 cups	=	1 pint; 16 fluid ounces
4 cups	=	2 pints; 1 quart; 32 fluid ounces

Pints, Quarts, Gallons and Pounds

1/2 pint	=	1 cup; 8 fluid ounces
1 pint	=	2 cups; 16 fluid ounces
1 quart	=	4 cups; 32 fluid ounces
1 gallon	=	4 quarts; 16 cups
1/4 pound	=	4 ounces
1/2 pound	=	8 ounces
3/4 pound	=	12 ounces
1 pound	=	16 ounces

Metric Volume Conversions

1 milliliter	=	1/5 teaspoon
5 milliliters	=	1 teaspoon
15 milliliters	=	1 tablespoon
60 milliliters	=	1/4 cup; 2 fluid ounces
80 milliliters	=	1/3 cup
125 milliliters	=	1/2 cup; 4 fluid ounces
160 milliliters	=	2/3 cup
180 milliliters	=	3/4 cup; 6 fluid ounces
250 milliliters	=	1 cup; 8 fluid ounces
375 milliliters	=	1-1/2 cups; 12 fluid ounces

500 milliliters=	2 cups; 16 fluid ounces; 1 pint
700 milliliters=	3 cups
950 milliliters=	4 cups; 32 fluid ounces; 1 quart
1 liter =	33.8 fluid ounces
3.8 liters =	4 quarts; 1 gallon

Metric Weight Conversions

1 gram   = .035 ounces
100 grams = 3.5 ounces
500 grams = 17.6 ounces; 1.1 pounds
1 kilogram = 35 ounces; 2.2 pounds

Cooking and Oven Temperature Conversions

0°C =	32°F
100°C =	212°F
120°C =	250°F
160°C =	320°F
180°C =	350°F
190°C =	375°F
205°C =	400°F
220°C =	425°F
230°C =	450°F

30 DAYS MEAL PLAN

	BREAKFAST	LUNCH	DINNER	SNACK OR DESSERT
WEEK 1				
Day 1	4. Protein Almond Muesli	26. Low sodium Salad with capers	120. Farfalle Pasta with Mushrooms	141. Tortilla Chips
Day 2	20. Italian Pizza Waffles	50. Mediterranean Moroccan Meatballs	41. Ground Beef Casserole	147. No-Bake Pumpkin Cheesecake
Day 3	15.Cinnamon Chia Pudding	36. Turmeric Roasted Cauliflower	68. Sunflower Seed Pesto Chicken	138. Napolitan Bombs
Day 4	1. Nut and Seed Granola	117. Rosemary Pasta Shells	112.Spinach, Shrimp & Tangerine Bowl	148. Crusty Peanut Butter Bars
Day 5	5. Apple Cinnamon Chia	21. Roman Tuna Salad	51.Saucy Beef Skillet	54. Tater Tot nachos
Day 6	6. Apple Almond Coconut Bowl	56. Cheese Stuffed Bacon Burger	64. Spicy Turkey Stir Fry	149. Pumpkin and Date Ice Cream
Day 7	19. Pork Cracklins with Eggs	77. Prawn Mexicana	63. Turkey Squash Scramble	158 Unbaked Brownie Balls
WEEK 2				
Day 8	10.Fibre Packed Oat and Walnut Muesli	24. Leftover turkey taco salad	82. Shrimp and Scallop Combo	52. Cheeseburger Muffins
Day 9	3. Nutmeg-Spiced Quinoa Porridge	115. Barley vegetable soup	48. Slow cooker braised oxtails	132. Olive pizza bombs
Day 10	18. Quick Oats with Coconut Milk	69. Hearty Cauliflower Rice with chicken	123. Snow Peas & Spaghetti	144. Corndog Muffins
Day 11	2. Mediterranean Golden Breakfast	127. Cheddar and Bell Pepper Pizza	49. Perfect Ribeye Steak	139. Coconut Orange Creamsicle Bombs
Day 12	15.Cinnamon Chia Pudding	108. Asparagus and Zucchini Pasta	89. Black pepper peach and salmon	145. Layered Fried Queso Blanco
Day 13	8. Raisin Nut & Sunflower Cereal	55. Pulled pork Sandwiches	121. Tortellini Salad with spinach	129. Ham and cheese stromboli
Day 14	9. Spicy Sweet Potato Breakfast Bowl	91. Sumac Cod in tomato Sauce	114. Fall pumpkin Soup	158. Unbaked Brownie balls
WEEK 3				

Day 15	14. Cinnamon Quinoa with Peach & Pecan	126. Tomato and Cauliflower Spaghetti	113. Coral Lentil & Swiss Chard Soup	160. Chocolatey Spinach brownies
Day 16	11. Healthy Flax Granola	100. Stir-fried vegetables & Rice	73. Seared Chicken & Tomatoes	150. Frozen fruity desert
Day 17	16. Walnut and Almond Porridge	29. Cheesy lemon quinoa salad	83. Orange poached salmon	139. Coconut Orange creamsicle bombs
Day 18	19.Pork Cracklins with Eggs	104.Kale slaw with creamy dressing	44. Asian grilled short ribs	154. Very spicy pumpkin pie
Day 19	7. Pecan Porridge with Banana	133. Tofu & Capers pizza	125. Vegetable Mediterranean pasta	58. BBQ Bacon wrapped smokies
Day 20	2. Mediterranean Golden Breakfast	110. Mediterraean Ratatouille	105. Aubergine mediterranean chili	147. No-bake pumpkin cheesecake
Day 21	13. Crisp Coconut Almond Granola	95. Seabass with Vegetables	53. Italian Stuffed Meatballs	141. Tortilla Chips
WEEK 4			
Day 22	6. Apple Almond Coconut Bowl	131. Rotisserie chicken pizza	97. Pinto & red bean chili	66. Turkey Stuffed boats
Day 23	15. Cinnamon Chia Pudding	64. Spicy Turkey stir-fry	45. Crispy Sesame beef	135. Pizza Breadsticks
Day 24	9. Spicy Sweet Potato Breakfast	101. Split peas wuith spinach	107. Broccoli cauliflower fry	67. Taco lettuce cups
Day 25	12. Blueberry Cinnamon Breakfast	57. Pigs in a blannket	102. Lemon pasta with broccoli	142. Jalapeno popper bombs
Day 26	17. Cinnamon Millet Porridge	30. Arugula & pear salad with walnuts	42. Delish seared ribeye stek	146. Berry and almond fruit wrap
Day 27	6. Apple Almond Coconut Bowl	61. Roasteed Lemon herb chicken	74. Sheet pan Fajitas	153.Citrusy Strawberry Soufflé
Day 28	7 .Pecan Porridge with Banana	71. Sweet potato chicken dumplings	122. Egg noodles with croutons	109. Veggie-Stuffed Tomatoes
WEEK 5			
Day 29	11 .Healthy Flax Granola	47. Bacon cheeseburger Casserole	99. Edamame Donburi	148. Crusty peanut butter bars
Day 30	9. Spicy Sweet Potato Breakfast	28. Farro Salad with Sweet pea pesto	46.Velveeta and Ground beef dinner	130. Mini Portobello pizzas

1. Nut and Seed Granola

Total Prep Time: 10 Minutes | Total Cook Time: 35 Minutes | Makes: 2 Servings

INGREDIENTS:
1 cup cashews
1/4 cup pumpkin seeds, shelled
1/2 cup coconut flakes
1/4 cup sunflower seeds
1/4 cup coconut oil
3/4 cup almonds
a few drops of stevia
1 teaspoon vanilla
Pinch low sodium salt

DIRECTIONS:
Preheat the oven to 300 degrees Fahrenheit. Using parchment paper, line a baking sheet. In a blender, pulse the cashews, almonds, coconut flakes, and pumpkin seeds to break them up into smaller bits.
Melt the coconut oil, vanilla, and stevia in a large microwave-safe bowl for 1 minute.
Stir in the sunflower seeds and the mixture from the blender to coat. Bake for 30 minutes.
To get a flat, even surface, press the granola mixture together. Let cool for 15 minutes before breaking into pieces.

Calories 288.0 | Total Fat 24.3 g | Saturated Fat 6.6 g | Cholesterol 0.0 mg | Sodium 19.4 mg | Potassium 252.3 mg | Carbohydrate 15.9 g | Dietary Fiber 3.9 g | Sugars 8.2 g | Protein 6.0 g

2. Mediterranean Golden Breakfast

Total Prep Time: 10 Minutes | Total Cook Time: 45 Minutes | Makes: 2 Servings

INGREDIENTS:
2 tablespoons coconut oil, melted
1/2 cup Flax-Meal, golden
1/2 cup Chia seed
2 tablespoons dark ground cinnamon
1 tablespoon hemp protein powder
a few drops of stevia
1 teaspoon vanilla extract
3/4 cup hot water

DIRECTIONS:
Start spreading the dough out onto a parchment paper-lined cookie sheet until it's extremely thin. Bake for 45 minutes. Pull out the sheet and cut it before dropping it. Replace it in the oven in the same condition as before, without separating the pieces. Serve with almond milk if desired.

Calories 371 | Total Fat 16.5g | Saturated Fat 4.6g | Sodium 875mg | Total Carbs 20g | Dietary Fiber 5g | Total Sugars 3g | Protein 39g

3. Nutmeg-Spiced Quinoa Porridge

Total Prep Time: 10 Minutes | Total Cook Time: 15 Minutes | Makes: 4 Servings

INGREDIENTS:
2 cups of water
1 cup uncooked red quinoa, cooked
½ teaspoon vanilla extract
½ cup coconut milk
¼ teaspoon fresh lemon zest, finely grated
10-12 drops of liquid stevia
1 teaspoon ground cinnamon
½ teaspoon ground ginger
½ teaspoon ground nutmeg
Pinch of ground cloves
2 tablespoons almonds, chopped

DIRECTIONS:
Combine quinoa and vanilla extract.
Add the coconut milk, lemon zest, stevia, and spices to the skillet with the quinoa and stir.
Remove the quinoa from the heat and fluff it with a fork right away.
Divide the quinoa mixture evenly among serving bowls.
Serve with a garnish of chopped almonds.

Calories: 248 | Fat: 11.4g | Carbs: 30.5g | Fiber: 4.4g | Sugars: 1.3g | Protein: 7.4g

4. Protein Almond Muesli

Total Prep Time: 10 Minutes | Makes: 2 Servings

INGREDIENTS:
1/2 teaspoon cinnamon
1 tablespoon raw almonds
1 cup unsweetened unsulfured coconut flakes
1 tablespoon chopped walnuts
1 tablespoon dark no-sugar-added chocolate chips
1 cup unsweetened almond milk
1 scoop of hemp protein

DIRECTIONS:
Toss together the coconut flakes, walnuts, almonds, and chocolate chips in a medium mixing dish.
Sprinkle cinnamon on top.
Douse the muesli with cold almond milk and devour with a spoon.

Calories: 399 | Fat 8.20g | Carbohydrates 64.50g | Sugar 11.30g | Fibre 6.6g | Protein 20.30g

5. Apple Cinnamon Chia

Total Prep Time: 10 Minutes | Makes: 2 Servings

INGREDIENTS:
1/2 chopped dried apple
2 cups chia seeds
1 cup hemp hearts
2 tablespoons real cinnamon
1 teaspoon low sodium salt
1/2c chopped nuts of your choi

DIRECTIONS:
Combine all of the ingredients in a jar, stir well, and keep in a cool, dry area.
Add a few drops of stevia to each serving.

Calories: 233 | protein 4.8g | carbohydrates 27.7g | dietary fiber10.1g | sugars 14.4g | fat 12.7g | saturated fat 1.1g

6. Apple Almond Coconut Bowl

Total Prep Time: 10 Minutes | Makes: 2 Servings

INGREDIENTS:
Pinch of cinnamon
one-half apple cored and roughly diced
a handful of sliced almonds
a handful of unsweetened coconut
1 pinch of low sodium salt

DIRECTIONS:
Combine all of the ingredients in a jar, stir well, and keep in a cool, dry area.
Add a few drops of stevia to each serving.

Calories 160 | Total Fat 12g | Saturated fat 4.5g | Sodium 60mg | Potassium 144mg | Carbohydrates 12g | Sugar 8g | Fiber 3g | Protein 3g

7. Pecan Porridge with Banana

Total Prep Time: 10 Minutes | Makes: 2 Servings

INGREDIENTS
½ cup soaked pecans
¾ cup boiling water
½ very ripe banana
a few drops of a few drops of stevia
2 tablespoons coconut butter
½ teaspoon cinnamon
⅛ teaspoon sea salt

DIRECTIONS
Blend everything until smooth and creamy. In a small saucepan, cook the mixture over medium-low heat.

Calories Per Serving: 290 | Total Fat 19g | Cholesterol 0mg | Sodium 10mg | Total Carbohydrates 28g | Sugars 18g | Protein 6g

8. Raisin Nut and Sunflower Seed Cereal

Total Prep Time: 10 Minutes | Total Cook Time: 35 Minutes | Makes: 2 Servings

INGREDIENTS
1 cup almonds, chopped
1 1/3 cup coconut
1/2 cup sunflower seeds
1/4 cup pumpkin seeds
2 tablespoons squash seeds
1/2 cup almond meal
1 1/2 teaspoon cinnamon
3 tablespoons coconut oil
1/4 cup raw honey
1 teaspoon vanilla
1 cup raisins

DIRECTIONS
Preheat the oven to 350 degrees. Combine all dry ingredients (except raisins). Warm the coconut oil and honey just enough to combine them smoothly.
Over the dry ingredients, pour the oil, honey, and vanilla extract. Combine thoroughly.
Pour into a baking sheet and bake for 25 minutes. Remove from the oven, stir, and return to the oven for another 6 minutes. Cool. Serve with homemade coconut milk or homemade almond milk with raisins! Keep the container sealed.

Calories 180 | Total Fat 3g grams | Saturated Fat 1g grams | Carbohydrates 40g grams | Dietary Fiber 6g grams | Sugars 14g grams | Protein 4g

9. Spicy Sweet Potato Breakfast Bowl

Total Prep Time: 10 Minutes | Total Cook Time: 26 Minutes | Makes: 4 Servings

INGREDIENTS
Pinch Salt and pepper
1 teaspoon chili powder
1/2 bell pepper, diced
2 sweet potatoes, peeled and diced
1/2 onion, diced
Extra virgin olive oil
1/2 red bell pepper, diced
1 jalapeño, chopped
2-3 cups fresh spinach
2 eggs
1 avocado, sliced
1 teaspoon ghee
2 strips bacon

DIRECTIONS
Preheat the oven to 375 degrees Fahrenheit (190 degrees Celsius). On a rimmed baking sheet, drizzle olive oil over the diced sweet potatoes. Season with salt, pepper, and chili powder. Bake for 20 minutes, rotating halfway through. Cook the bacon in a skillet over medium heat. Crumble on a paper towel-lined tray. Sauté the onion, bell peppers, and jalapeno in a skillet for 6 minutes, or until tender. Finally, add the spinach and cook until it has wilted fully. In a separate skillet, melt the ghee. Cook until the eggs are done to your satisfaction, seasoning with salt and pepper. Place the sweet potatoes in two separate dishes. The veggie mixture goes on top, followed by the egg, crumbled bacon, and avocado.

Calories 460 | Total Fat 23g grams | Saturated Fat 9g grams |Trans Fat 0g grams | Cholesterol 535mg milligrams | Sodium 1000mg milligrams | Total Carbohydrates 24g grams | Dietary Fiber 4g grams | Sugars 7g grams | Protein 40g grams

10. Fiber-Packed Oat and Walnut Muesli

Total Prep Time: 10 Minutes | Makes: 2 Servings

INGREDIENTS:
¼ cup hulled sunflower seeds
1 ½ cup rolled oats
1 ½ cups whole-wheat bran flakes
¼ cup chopped walnuts
½ cup raisins

DIRECTIONS
Toss everything together.

Calories: 323 | Total Fat: 12g | Saturated Fat: 1.2g | Unsaturated Fat: 9.3g | Total Carbohydrate: 51g | Dietary Fiber: 7g | Sugar: 16g | Protein: 10

11. Healthy Flax Granola

Total Prep Time: 10 Minutes | Total Cook Time: 35 Minutes | Makes: 16 Servings

INGREDIENTS:
1/4 cup coconut oil
3 cups rolled oats
3/4 cup walnuts, chopped
1 tablespoon ground flax seeds
1 banana, mashed
2 teaspoons cinnamon
1/2 cup pecans, chopped
2 teaspoons vanilla extract
1/3 cup pure maple syrup

DIRECTIONS:
Preheat the oven to 350 degrees Fahrenheit (180 degrees Celsius) Combine oats, walnuts, pecans, flax seeds, and cinnamon in a mixing dish. In a small saucepan over low heat, combine the coconut oil, maple syrup, and vanilla extract. Heat until all of the ingredients are well blended and the coconut oil has melted. Remove the pan from the heat and add the mashed bananas to it. Toss the banana mixture with the oats in a mixing dish and whisk to combine. Place the mixture on the baking sheet in a single layer. Bake for 35 minutes, flipping halfway through. Allow it cool completely before storing it in an airtight container.

Calories: 157 | 10g Fat | 18g Carbohydrates | 3g Protein

12. Blueberry Cinnamon Breakfast Bake

Total Prep Time: 10 Minutes | Total Cook Time: 28 Minutes | Makes: 2 Servings

INGREDIENTS:
2 eggs, beaten
8 slices of whole-wheat bread
3 cups blueberries
1 cup of low-fat milk
1/4 cup brown sugar, divided
Zest of 1 lemon, divided
2 teaspoons cinnamon, divided

DIRECTIONS:
Preheat the oven to 350 degrees Fahrenheit (180 degrees Celsius). Combine the eggs, milk, brown sugar, cinnamon, and lemon zest in a mixing bowl. In a mixing bowl, toss the bread and blueberries with the egg mixture and whisk until most of the liquid has been absorbed. Halfway fill muffin tins with batter. Combine 1 tablespoon brown sugar and 1 teaspoon cinnamon. Sprinkle the topping over the French toast cups. Cook for 18 minutes, or until the French toast is done and the top is browned. In a small saucepan, combine the remaining 1 cup of blueberries, lemon zest, and 1 tablespoon brown sugar and cook for 10 minutes, or until liquid is released. Crush blueberries and dollop the syrupy blueberry over the toasted French toast.

Calories: 170 | 3g Fat | 171mg Sodium | 30g Carbohydrates | 4g fiber | 15g Sugar | 7g Added | 7g Protein

13. Crisp Coconut Almond Granola

Total Prep Time: 10 Minutes | Total Cook Time: 37 Minutes | Makes: 2 Servings

INGREDIENTS:
1/4 cup sliced almonds
2 teaspoons vanilla extract
1 1/2 cups rolled oats
1/4 cup sunflower seeds
1/4 shredded coconut
1 teaspoon cinnamon
1/4 cup honey
2 tablespoons vegetable oil
1/4 cup raisins

DIRECTIONS:
Preheat the oven to 325 degrees Fahrenheit (165 degrees Celsius).
Combine oats, sunflower seeds, almonds, coconut, and cinnamon in a mixing bowl.
Add the honey, oil, and vanilla essence.
Spread the batter onto the baking sheet.
Bake for 30 minutes, or until gently browned.
Stir the mixture every 7 minutes to ensure that it cooks evenly and without burning.
Toss in the raisins once the granola has cooled.

Calories: 134 | 6g Fat | 1g Saturated | 0mg Cholesterol, 13mg Sodium | 17g Carbohydrates | 2g fiber | 8.5g Sugar | 5g Added | 2g Protein

14. Cinnamon Quinoa with Peach & Pecan

Total Prep Time: 10 Minutes | Total Cook Time: 2 Hours | Makes: 6 Servings

INGREDIENTS:
Cooking spray
2 ½ cups water
1 cup uncooked quinoa, rinsed, drained
½ teaspoon ground cinnamon
1 ½ cups fat-free half-and-half
¼ cup sugar
1½ teaspoons vanilla extract
2 cups frozen, unsweetened peach slices
¼ cup chopped pecans, dry-roasted

DIRECTIONS
Using cooking spray, lightly coat the interior of a slow cooker. Add some water. In a mixing dish, combine the quinoa and cinnamon. Cook for 2 hours on low, or until the quinoa is mushy and the water has been absorbed.
Just before serving the quinoa, mix the half-and-half, sugar, and vanilla essence in a separate dish until the sugar has dissolved. Place the quinoa into dishes to serve. On top of that, place the peaches. Mix the half-and-half and pour it in. Garnish with pecans.

Calories: 250 | Total Fat: 7 g | Saturated Fat: .5 g | Sodium: 65 Mg | Total Carbohydrate: 42 g | Dietary Fiber: 4 g | Sugar: 17 g | Protein: 10 g

15. Cinnamon Chia Pudding

Total Prep Time: 10 Minutes | Makes: 4 Servings

INGREDIENTS:
1/3 cup chia seeds
1½ cups almond milk
½ cup pumpkin puree
2 tablespoons of raw honey
1/8 teaspoon cloves
2 tablespoons almond butter
1 teaspoon vanilla extract
1 protein powder sachet
¼ teaspoon nutmeg powder
1 teaspoon cinnamon powder
1/8 teaspoon ginger
pinch of salt

DIRECTIONS:
Blitz everything in a blender, except the chia seeds.
Add the chia seeds and mix well.
Refrigerate overnight before serving.

Calories: 363 | Fat: 29g | Carbs: 22.3g | Fiber: 6.6g | Sugars: 13.4g | Protein: 11.2g

16. Walnut and Almond Porridge

Total Prep Time: 15 Minutes | Total Cook Time: 25 Minutes | Makes: 5 Servings

INGREDIENTS:
½ cup pecans
½ cup almonds
¼ cup sunflower seeds
¼ cup chia seeds
¼ cup coconut flakes(unsweetened)
4 cups almond milk(unsweetened)
½ teaspoon cinnamon powder
¼ teaspoon ginger powder
1 teaspoon powdered stevia
1 tablespoon almond butter

DIRECTIONS:
In a food processor, combine pecans, almonds, and sunflower seeds.
Bring the nut mixture, chia seeds, coconut flakes, almond milk, spices, and stevia powder to a boil for about 20 minutes.
Serve with a dollop of almond butter.

Calories: 292 | Fat: 7.5g | Carbs: 9.6g | Fiber: 6.5g | Sugars: 1.2g | Protein: 8g

17. Cinnamon Millet Porridge

Total Prep Time: 10 Minutes | Total Cook Time: 10 Minutes | Makes: 4 Servings

INGREDIENTS:
1 tablespoon coconut butter
1 teaspoon ginger powder
2 teaspoons ground cinnamon
½ teaspoon ground cloves
1½ cups finely ground millet
1½ cups of water
4 cups unsweetened coconut
milk

DIRECTIONS:
In a skillet over medium-high heat, melt the coconut oil and
brown the spices for about 30 seconds.
Add millet and stir to combine.
Bring the water and coconut milk to a boil, stirring
constantly.
Reduce heat to low and simmer, partially covered, for about
10-15 minutes, or until desired thickness, stirring
occasionally.
Serve with desired garnish.

Calories: 398 | Fat: 11.7g | Carbs: 63.1g | Fiber: 7.1g |
Sugars: 6.1g | Protein: 9.4g

18. Quick Oats with Coconut Milk

Total Prep Time: 10 Minutes | Total Cook Time: 3 Minutes | Makes: 2 Servings

INGREDIENTS:
2/3 cup unsweetened coconut
milk
½ cup gluten-free quick-
cooking rolled oats
½ teaspoon ground cinnamon
½ teaspoon ground turmeric
¼ teaspoon ground ginger

DIRECTIONS:
In a microwave-safe bowl, combine milk and oats and
microwave on high for about 45 seconds.
Mix in the spices.
Microwave for 2 minutes, stirring after 20 seconds.

Calories: 121 | Fat: 3.2g | Carbs: 17.8g | Fiber: 3g | Sugars:
2.5g | Protein: 3.9g

19. Pork Cracklins with Eggs

Total Prep Time: 10 Minutes | Total Cook Time: 10 Minutes | Makes: 3 Servings

INGREDIENTS
4 slices Bacon, cooked
5 Eggs
5 oz. Pork Rinds
1 Tomato
1 Avocado
2 Jalapeno Peppers, de-seeded
1 Onion
1/4 cup Cilantro, chopped
Salt and Pepper to Taste

DIRECTIONS
In the bacon fat, fry pork rinds.
Add the vegetables to the skillet once the pig rinds are crispy.
Combine all of the ingredients in a mixing bowl and season to taste.
Add chopped cilantro to the pan once the onions are almost transparent.
Mix everything in the pan with 5 pre-scrambled eggs.
Season with salt and pepper as needed.
Allow to cook like an omelet, then mix once to allow the uncooked egg to settle to the bottom of the pan.
Just before serving, dice an avocado and fold it into the mixture.

Calories 421 | 43g Fats | 5g Carbohydrates | 27g Protein

20. Italian Pizza Waffles

Total Prep Time: 10 Minutes| Total Cook Time: 4 Minutes| Makes: 2 Servings

INGREDIENTS
4 Eggs
4 tablespoons Parmesan Cheese
3 tablespoons Almond Flour
1 tablespoon Psyllium Husk Powder
1 tablespoon Bacon Grease
1 teaspoon Baking Powder
1 teaspoon Italian Seasoning
Salt and Pepper to Taste
1/2 cup Tomato Sauce
3 oz. Cheddar Cheese
14 slices Pepperoni

DIRECTIONS
In a container, combine all ingredients, excluding tomato sauce and cheese, using an immersion blender.
Preheat your waffle iron and pour half of the batter into it.
Allow cooking for a few minutes.
Top each waffle with tomato sauce and cheese.
Then, in the oven, broil for 4 minutes.
Add pepperoni on the top of them if desired.

Calories: 526 | 45g Fats | 5g Carbohydrates | 29g Protein

21. Roman Tuna Salad

Total Prep Time: 10 Minutes | Makes: 2 Servings

INGREDIENTS:
10 sun-dried tomatoes
1/2 Tablespoon lemon juice
1-2 ribs of celery, diced finely
2 Tablespoons of extra virgin olive oil
3 Tablespoons finely chopped parsley
1 clove of garlic, minced
2 (5 oz.) cans of tuna, flaked
Pinch low sodium salt and pepper

DIRECTIONS:
In a skillet, heat oil and add the chicken; cook until the liquid has evaporated, stirring in the water and taco seasoning.
Prepare all of your toppings by shredding, chopping, and dicing them.
Combine lettuce, toppings, chicken, remaining oil and vinegar dressing, and smashed chips in a salad bowl.

Calories 292.5 |Total Fat 6.0 g | Saturated Fat 1.8 g | Polyunsaturated Fat 0.3 g | Monounsaturated Fat 0.1 g | Cholesterol 59.6 mg | Sodium 1,198.7 mg | Potassium 634.2 mg | Total Carbohydrate 29.2 g | Dietary Fiber 7.2 g | Sugars 3.3 g | Protein 31.1 g

22. Healthy Turkey and Onion Salad

Total Prep Time: 10 Minutes | Total Cook Time: 40 Minutes | Makes: 16 Servings

INGREDIENTS:
FOR TURKEY:
1 lb. boneless turkey breasts
Pinch Low sodium salt and pepper
1 tablespoon olive oil
FOR THE SALSA:
1 small bunch of cilantro leaves
1 large tomato, quartered
1/2 red onion, cut into large chunks
Juice of 1 lime
Pinch low sodium salt and pepper
1 garlic clove, peele

DIRECTIONS:
On a baking sheet, bake turkey breasts coated in olive oil for 35 minutes, at 350 degrees. In a food processor, add all salsa ingredients and pulse until finely chopped. Take the turkey out of the oven and set it aside to cool. After each breast has cooled enough to handle, break it into three or four smaller pieces and place them in the food processor. Using the chopping blade, pulsate until shredded.Toss the turkey with the salsa in a mixing dish and combine thoroughly with a fork. Set aside for at least two hours in the refrigerator.

Calories: 105 | Sugar 5 g | Sodium: 301.6 mg | Fat: 7.3 g | Carbohydrates: 10.2 g | Protein: 1.4 g | Cholesterol: 0 mg

23. Garlicky Rucola Salad

Total Prep Time: 10 Minutes | Makes: 2 Servings

INGREDIENTS:
1 bunch of cilantro, chopped
5-6 Roma tomatoes, diced
1 small chili pepper, sliced
2 ripe avocados, sliced
1 small yellow onion, diced
a handful of rucola leaf

DIRECTIONS:
In a large mixing dish, pour the lemon juice. Whisk in the oil gradually.
Season with pepper and low-sodium salt.
Toss in the greens until uniformly coated and serve right away.

Calories: 3 | Sugar 5 g | Sodium: 301.6 mg | Fat: 7.3 g | Carbohydrates: 10.2 g | Protein: 1.4 g | Cholesterol: 0 mg

24. Leftover Turkey Taco Salad

Total Prep Time: 10 Minutes | Makes: 2 Servings

INGREDIENTS:
1 tablespoon coconut or olive oil
1/2 lbs. leftover turkey, cooked and chopped
1 1/2 tablespoons taco seasoning
1/4 cup water
1 tablespoon of rice vinegar
Shredded lettuce
TACO SEASONING:
3 tablespoons of chili powder
2 teaspoons of paprika
1 teaspoon garlic powder
1 teaspoon of red pepper flakes
1 teaspoon onion powder
1 teaspoon oregano
2 teaspoons cumin
4 teaspoons of low sodium salt

TOPPINGS
Red Onion
Sliced Olives
Tomatoes
Avocado
Bell Peppers
Crushed Sweet Potato Chips
DIRECTIONS:
In a skillet, heat oil and add the chicken; cook until the liquid has evaporated, stirring in the water and taco seasoning.Prepare all of your toppings by shredding, chopping, and dicing them. Combine lettuce, toppings, chicken, remaining oil and vinegar dressing, and smashed chips in a salad bowl.

Calories 292.5 | Total Fat 6.0 g | Saturated Fat 1.8 g | Polyunsaturated Fat 0.3 g | Monounsaturated Fat 0.1 g | Cholesterol 59.6 mg | Sodium 1,198.7 mg | Potassium 634.2 mg | Total Carbohydrate 29.2 g | Dietary Fiber 7.2 g | Sugars 3.3 g | Protein 31.1 g

25. Simple Salsa Salad

Total Prep Time: 10 Minutes| Makes: 2 Servings

INGREDIENTS:
1 bunch of cilantro, chopped
5-6 Roma tomatoes, diced
1 small chili pepper, sliced
2 ripe avocados, sliced
1 small yellow onion, diced
a handful of rucola leaf

DIRECTIONS:
Toss ingredients in a mixing bowl.

18 calories| protein 0.8g| carbohydrates 4.1g|dietary fiber 1.1g| sugars 2.5g| fat 0.2g|calcium 10.8mg| iron 0.2mg| magnesium 9.6mg| potassium 196.1mg| sodium 120.8mg

26. Low Sodium Salad with Capers

Total Prep Time: 10 Minutes| Makes: 2 Servings

INGREDIENTS:
5 cups of any salad greens
DRESSING:
1/2 cup olive oil
3 tablespoons lemon juice
Pinch low sodium salt and pepper
1 tablespoon pure mustard powder
3 tablespoons capers, minced

DIRECTIONS:
Combine the oil, lemon juice, and mustard in a mixing bowl.
Add veggies and mix thoroughly.
Capers, low sodium salt, and pepper are added.
Toss the salad with the dressing and serve.

VCalories: 366 |Fat 35g|Saturated fat: 4g |Unsaturated fat: 29g |Trans fat: 0g |Carbohydrates: 10g |Sugar: 3g |Sodium: 305mg |Fiber: 3g |Protein: 5g |Cholesterol: 8mg

27. Mixed Green Salad with Beets

Total Prep Time: 10 Minutes| Total Cook Time: 34 Minutes| Makes: 3 Servings

INGREDIENTS:
1/3 cup reduced-fat feta cheese, crumbled
2 medium beets, tops trimmed
1/8 teaspoon salt
2 tablespoons calcium-fortified orange juice
1 1/2 teaspoon honey
1 orange, segmented
2 tablespoons raw, hulled sunflower seeds
1/8 teaspoon black pepper
1/4 cup olive oil
3 cups packed mixed salad greens

DIRECTIONS:
Bring beets to a boil and cook until fork-tender, about 30 minutes.
Under running water, peel them and cut them into wedges.
Mix the orange juice, honey, garlic, salt, and pepper in a mixing bowl.
Whisk in the olive oil until the dressing is smooth.
In a small sauté pan over medium-low heat, melt the butter and toast sunflower seeds for 3 minutes, or until aromatic.
Combine beets, sunflower seeds, orange segments, mixed greens, and feta cheese in a large serving bowl.
Drizzle with the dressing.

220 Calories, 16g Fat (3g Saturated), 8mg Cholesterol, 227mg Sodium, 14g Carbohydrates (3g fiber, 10g Sugar), 4g Protein

28. Farro Salad with Sweet Pea Pesto

Total Prep Time: 10 Minutes| Makes: 8 Servings

INGREDIENTS:
1/4 cup parmesan cheese
1 cup farro, cooked and cooled
1 1/2 cup frozen peas, defrosted
2 cloves garlic
1 teaspoon black pepper
1/2 cup low-sodium canned white beans
1/4 cup olive oil
2 tablespoons sunflower seeds, Hulled
Zest of 1 lemon
1 bell pepper, diced
2 cups cherry or grape tomatoes

DIRECTIONS:
In a food processor, combine peas, parmesan, garlic, sunflower seeds, and pepper.
Pulse until the peas are finely minced and all of the ingredients are properly mixed. Slowly drip in the olive oil.
Combine farro, pesto sauce, white beans, tomatoes, bell pepper, and lemon zest in a large mixing dish.

200 Calories, 10g Fat 2g Saturated, 2mg Cholesterol, 86mg Sodium, 23g Carbohydrates 5g fiber, 4g Sugar, 0g Added, 7g Protein

29. Cheesy Lemon Quinoa Salad

Total Prep Time: 10 Minutes| Makes: 4 Servings

INGREDIENTS:
2 tablespoons olive oil
Juice of 1/2 lemon
1 cup quinoa, cooked
2 cloves garlic, minced
Pinch teaspoon salt
1 small yellow bell pepper,
diced
1 teaspoon black pepper
1 cucumber diced
1 tablespoon dill, chopped
1 cup reduced-fat feta cheese,
crumbled
1 cup cherry tomatoes,
quartered

DIRECTIONS:
For the dressing: Combine olive oil, garlic, lemon juice, salt, and pepper in a dish.
Combine the cooled quinoa, cherry tomatoes, bell pepper, cucumber, feta cheese, and dill with the dressing.

250 Calories, 9g Fat (4g Saturated), 17mg Cholesterol, 262mg Sodium, 33g Carbohydrates (5g fiber, 4g Sugar, 0g Added), 9g Protein

30. Arugula & Pear Salad with Walnuts

Total Prep Time: 10 Minutes| Total Cook Time: 4 Minutes| Makes: 8 Servings

INGREDIENTS
SALAD
4 cups arugula, trimmed,
washed, and dried
2 firm red Bartlett pears
½ cup chopped walnuts
5 cups butterhead lettuce
DRESSING
2 tablespoons minced shallot
½ teaspoon Dijon mustard
1 ½ tablespoon balsamic
vinegar
3 tablespoons vegetable broth
Pinch freshly ground pepper
3 tablespoons extra-virgin olive
oil ¼ teaspoon salt

DIRECTIONS
Combine the shallot, broth, oil, vinegar, mustard, salt, and pepper in a small mixing dish. To make the salad, toast the walnuts for 2 minutes in a dry skillet over medium-low heat, rotating often. Cut each pear into 16 wedges just before serving. Half-fill a big mixing bowl with water. Toss with 1 tablespoon of the dressing to coat. In a mixing bowl, combine the lettuce, arugula, and remaining dressing. Top with walnuts and serve.

Calories: 125, Total Fat: 8 g, Saturated Fat: 1 g, Unsaturated Fat: 8 g, Cholesterol: 0, Mg Sodium: 104 Mg, Total Carbohydrates: 10 g, Fiber: 3 g, Sugar: 5 g, Protein: 2 g

31. Mushrooms & Spinach

Total Prep Time: 15 Minutes| Total Cook Time: 15 Minutes| Makes: 3 Servings

INGREDIENTS:
1 teaspoon coconut oil
5-6 mushrooms, sliced
2 tablespoons olive oil
½ red onion, sliced
1 clove of garlic, minced
½ teaspoon fresh lemon zest, finely grated
¼ cup cherry tomatoes, sliced
Pinch of ground nutmeg
3 cups fresh spinach, shredded
½ Tablespoons fresh lemon juice
Pinch Salt
Pinch ground black pepper

DIRECTIONS:
Heat the coconut oil and sauté the mushrooms for about 4 minutes.
Heat the olive oil and cook the onion for about 3 minutes.
Add the garlic, lemon zest and tomatoes, salt, and black pepper and cook for about 2-3 minutes, lightly crushing the tomatoes with a spatula.
Cook for about 2-3 minutes after adding the spinach.
Stir in mushrooms and lemon juice and remove from heat.

Calories: 179| Fat: 16.8g | Carbs: 7.3g | Fiber: 2.4g| Sugars: 2.9g | Protein: 3.4g

32. Sautéed Apples with Ginger

Total Prep Time: 10 Minutes| Total Cook Time: 10 Minutes| Makes: 4 Servings

INGREDIENTS:
3 apples, peeled, cored, and sliced
1 tablespoon grated fresh ginger
4 oz. Stevia powder
1 teaspoon ground cinnamon
pinch of sea salt
2 tablespoons coconut oil

DIRECTIONS:
In a nonstick skillet over medium-high heat, heat the coconut oil until simmering.
Toss in the ginger, apple, cinnamon, stevia, and salt.
Cook, stirring periodically, for 7 to 10 minutes, or until the apples are soft.

Calories: 152| total fat: 7 g | Total carbs: 24g | sugar: 18g | fiber: 5g | protein: 1g

33. Black Pepper Citrusy Spinach

Total Prep Time: 10 Minutes| Total Cook Time: 7 Minutes| Makes: 4 Servings

INGREDIENTS:
2 tablespoons olive oil (extra-virgin)
2 garlic cloves, crushed
Juice of 1 orange
zest of 1 orange
3 cups fresh baby spinach
1 teaspoon sea salt
⅛ teaspoon black pepper, freshly ground

DIRECTIONS:
Heat the olive oil in a skillet over high heat until it begins to simmer.
Cook, stirring periodically, for 3 minutes after adding the spinach and garlic.
Add orange juice, orange zest, salt, and pepper.
Cook, stirring constantly until juices have evaporated, about 4 minutes.

Calories: 80| total fat: 7 g | Total carbohydrates: 4g | sugar: 2 g| fiber: 1g| Protein: 1g

34. Rosemary Sweet Potatoes

Total Prep Time: 10 Minutes| Total Cook Time: 15 Minutes| Makes: 4 Servings

INGREDIENTS:
2 tablespoons olive oil (extra-virgin)
2 sweet potatoes, cut into ½-inch cubes
1 tablespoon chopped fresh rosemary leaves
½ teaspoons sea salt
3 garlic cloves, crushed
¼ teaspoon black pepper, freshly ground

DIRECTIONS:
Heat the olive oil until simmering.
Toss in the sweet potatoes, rosemary, and salt.
Cook, stirring until the sweet potatoes begin to brown.
Add garlic and pepper. Cook 30 seconds, stirring constantly.

Calories: 199| total fat: 7 g | Total carbohydrates: 33 g| Sugar: 1g| fiber: 5g | Protein: 2g

35. Almond Balsamic Beans

Total Prep Time: 10 Minutes| Total Cook Time: 15 Minutes| Makes: 4 Servings

INGREDIENTS:
1 pound cleaned green beans
1 tablespoon olive oil
2 tablespoons ground almonds
1½ tablespoons balsamic vinegar

DIRECTIONS:
Steam the green beans with olive oil and balsamic vinegar. Add the slivered almonds just before the desired doneness is reached.
Remove from heat and serve.

Calories: 316|Fat: 27g|Saturated Fat: 3g|Carbohydrates: 15g|Fiber: 6g|Protein: 8g

36. Turmeric Roasted Cauliflower

Total Prep Time: 20 Minutes| Total Cook Time: 10 Minutes| Makes: 5 Servings

INGREDIENTS:
2 teaspoons lemon juice
3 tablespoons olive oil (extra-virgin)
½ teaspoon ground cumin
½ teaspoon of salt
2 teaspoons ground turmeric
½ teaspoon ground pepper
2 large garlic cloves, crushed
8 cups cauliflower florets

DIRECTIONS:
Preheat the oven to 425 degrees Fahrenheit.
Whisk together oil, turmeric, cumin, salt, pepper, and garlic in a bowl. Add cauliflower and stir. Place on a large rimmed baking sheet.
Roast until golden brown and tender.
Drizzle the lemon juice on top.

124 calories| Protein 3.5g| carbohydrates 9.6 g | dietary fiber 3.7g | sugar 3.3g| fat 8.9g | saturated fat 1.4g

37. Mediterranean Spinach Potatoes

Total Prep Time: 10 Minutes| Total Cook Time: 1 hour 35 Minutes| Makes: 8 Servings

INGREDIENTS:
4 medium russet potatoes, washed
1 tablespoon olive oil, extra-virgin
1-pound fresh spinach, chopped
3 garlic cloves, crushed
1 tablespoon oregano
⅓ cup light cream cheese
1 cup onion, diced
1 teaspoon ground pepper
1 teaspoon kosher salt
1 cup crumbled feta cheese

DIRECTIONS:
Preheat the oven to 400 degrees F.
Bake directly on the middle rack until tender, 50 to 60 minutes. Meanwhile, in a large saucepan over medium-high heat, heat the oil. Add onion and cook, stirring occasionally, until onion is soft, 2 to 4 minutes. Add the spinach, garlic, and oregano. Cook, stirring constantly, until the mixture is hot, about 4 minutes. In a 9 x 13-inch skillet, arrange the potato skins.
In a mixing dish, combine the cream cheese, pepper, and salt using a hand blender. Stir in spinach mixture and 1/2 cup feta. Fill each potato skin with about 3/4 cup filling. Sprinkle the remaining 1 tablespoon of feta on top.
Bake until topping is smoking and feta is golden brown, 25 to 35 minutes.

197 Calories| Protein 7.8g| Carbohydrates 24.2g | Dietary Fiber 3.7g | Sugar 3.1 g | Fat 8.3g | Saturated Fat 4.3g

38. Mediterranean Fried Spinach

Total Prep Time: 10 Minutes| Total Cook Time: 10 Minutes| Makes: 4 Servings

INGREDIENTS:
2 teaspoons olive oil (extra-virgin)
1 small onion, diced
1 clove of garlic, minced
1 pound frozen spinach leaves, sliced
Salt and freshly ground pepper to taste
¼ cup currants
3 tablespoons pine nuts, toasted
Balsamic vinegar, to taste

DIRECTIONS:
Heat the oil and then cook the onion and garlic.
Add spinach and cook, tossing periodically until spinach is heated through.
Stir in the currants, pine nuts, a dash of balsamic vinegar, salt, and pepper.

117 calories| protein 5.3g | carbs 14.2g | dietary fiber 4.4g | sugar 8g | fat 5.9g | saturated fat 0.6g

39. Roasted Carrots with Cumin

Total Prep Time: 1 Hour 15 Minutes| Total Cook Time: 30 Minutes| Makes: 8 Servings

INGREDIENTS:
¾ teaspoon salt
2 tablespoons olive oil (extra-virgin)
4 tablespoons melted coconut oil
2 teaspoons lime juice
½ teaspoon ground cumin
lemon zest and lemon juice of 1 lemon
¼ cup of honey
2 tablespoons cumin seeds, crushed
3 pounds carrots
Fresh chives and lime zest for garnish
2 teaspoons coriander seeds, crushed
½ cup nugget seeds
2 teaspoons smoked paprika
2 Tablespoons minced garlic plus 2 teaspoons
2 cups plain low-fat Greek yogurt
½ cup chopped fresh dill
½ teaspoon ground pepper
3 tablespoons light mayonnaise

DIRECTIONS:
Preheat the oven to 325°F.
Combine the Pepitas, half of the coconut oil, salt, and ground cumin, and then spread in an even layer on a pan. Bake for 12 minutes.
Heat the remaining coconut oil, honey, cumin, coriander seeds, paprika, and pepper in a small saucepan over medium heat -high.
Remove the pan from the heat and add garlic and lime juice.
Place carrots on a large baking sheet or rimmed skillet, pour over the honey mixture, and mix well. Spread in an even layer.
Roast the carrots, turning halfway through cooking, for about 40 minutes.
Whisk together the yogurt, dill, mayonnaise, olive oil, lemon zest, lemon juice, remaining 2 teaspoons of garlic, paprika, and salt.
Serve the carrots with the sauce and the Pepitas.

316 calories| fat 18g | carbohydrates 30g | dietary fiber 6g | Protein 10g | Saturated fatty acids 7g

40. Brussels, Carrot & Greens

Total Prep Time: 10 Minutes| Total Cook Time: 8 Minutes| Makes: 2 Servings

INGREDIENTS:
1 broccoli
2 carrots, sliced thin
6 brussels sprouts
2 cloves of garlic
1 teaspoon of caraway seeds
1/2 lemon
Peel 1 lemon Olive oil

DIRECTIONS:
Steam all the vegetables for 8 minutes on low heat.
Sauté garlic with caraway seeds, lemon peel, lemon juice, and olive oil.
Add the carrot and Brussels sprouts.

Calories 160| Fat 3g (Saturated 0g) | Cholesterol 0mg| Sodium 549mg| Carbohydrate 30g| Dietary Fiber 5g| Protein 8g.

41. Ground Beef Casserole

Total Prep Time: 15 Minutes| Total Cook Time: 50 Minutes| Makes: 6 Servings

INGREDIENTS
12-ounce package wide egg noodles
1 tablespoon ground cumin
1 lb. ground beef
1 teaspoon dried oregano
1 onion, chopped
1/2 teaspoon cayenne pepper
3 cloves garlic, minced
1 cup shredded sharp Cheddar cheese
2 (15 oz.) cans of tomato sauce
8-ounce can of tomato sauce
15 oz. water
1 cup red wine

DIRECTIONS
Before you do anything else, preheat the oven to 350 degrees F and butter a baking dish. Cook the egg noodles in a pot of lightly salted boiling water for about 5 minutes, stirring occasionally. Drain them thoroughly and set them away. Cook the beef in a skillet over. until it is thoroughly browned. Stir in the onion and garlic and cook until the onion is soft. Bring to a simmer the tomato sauce, wine, water, oregano, cumin, and cayenne pepper.
Stir in the pasta and transfer the mixture to the baking dish that has been prepared. Cook everything for about 20 minutes in the oven, topped with cheddar cheese.

Calories 510 kcal, Fat 20 g, Carbohydrates 49g, Protein 27.6 g

42. Delish Seared Rib-Eye Steak

Total Prep Time: 10 Minutes| Total Cook Time: 50 Minutes| Makes: 3 Servings

INGREDIENTS
2 Ribeye Steaks
3 tablespoons Bacon Fat
Salt and Pepper to Taste

DIRECTIONS
Preheat the oven to 250 degrees Fahrenheit. Place your steaks on top of a cookie sheet on a wire rack. Season with a generous amount of salt and pepper.
Preheat the oven to 400°F and bake for 45 minutes.
Allow the steaks to rest for a few minutes before serving.
In a cast-iron or ceramic cast-iron skillet, heat the bacon oil until the pan is very hot. I usually wait till the grease reaches its smoking point. Place the steaks in the pan and sear each side for 45 seconds.
Don't forget to brown the steak's sides!
Allow for 3 minutes of resting time before serving heated.

430 Calories, 37g Fats, 0g Carbohydrates, and 30.3g Protein.

43. Southwestern Pork Stew

Total Prep Time: 10 Minutes| Total Cook Time: 4 Hours 20 Minutes| Makes: 6 Servings

INGREDIENTS
1 lb. Cooked Pork Shoulder, sliced
2 teaspoon Chili Powder
2 teaspoon Cumin
1 teaspoon Minced Garlic
2 cups Chicken Broth
1/2 teaspoon salt
1/2 teaspoon Pepper
1 teaspoon Paprika
1 teaspoon Oregano
1/4 teaspoon Cinnamon
2 Bay Leafs
6 oz. Button Mushrooms
1/2 sliced Jalapeno
1/2 cup brewed coffee
1/2 Onion
1/2 Green Bell Pepper, sliced
1/2 Red Bell Pepper, sliced
Juice 1/2 Lime
2 cups Bone Broth
1/4 cup Tomato Paste

DIRECTIONS
Slicing and cutting all vegetables is a must. Allow the bone broth to warm up to room temperature. Heat Olive Oil in a pan over high heat and then add the vegetables and cook until they are slightly softened and fragrant. In a slow cooker, combine bone broth, chicken broth, and coffee.
Mix the meat and mushrooms in the slow cooker. In the slow cooker, combine the spices and veggies (along with the oil). Combine all ingredients, cover, and cook on low for 4 to 10 hours. Remove the lid and whisk everything together once it's done.

386 Calories, 29g Fats, 4g Carbohydrates, and 19g Protein.

44. Asian Grilled Short Ribs

Total Prep Time: 10 Minutes| Total Cook Time: 15 Minutes| Makes: 4 Servings

INGREDIENTS
RIBS AND MARINADE
2 tablespoons Fish Sauce
6 Short Ribs
1/4 cup Soy Sauce
2 tablespoons Rice Vinegar
ASIAN SPICE RUB
1 teaspoon Ground Ginger
1/4 teaspoon Cardamom
1/2 teaspoon Onion Powder
1/2 teaspoon Minced Garlic
1/2 teaspoon Sesame Seed
1/2 teaspoon Red Pepper Flakes
1 tablespoons Salt

DIRECTIONS
Combine the soy sauce, rice vinegar, and fish sauce in a mixing bowl.
Short ribs should be placed in a casserole dish or container with high edges. Allow 45-60 minutes for the marinade to sit on the ribs.
Combine the spice rub ingredients.
Pour the spice mixture evenly over both sides of the ribs after emptying the marinade from the casserole dish.
Preheat your grill and start cooking the ribs! Depending on thickness, around 5 minutes per side.
Serve with vegetables or a side dish of your choice.

417 Calories, 38g Fats, 0.9g Carbohydrates, and 25g Protein.

45. Crispy Sesame Beef

Total Prep Time: 10 Minutes| Total Cook Time: 15 Minutes| Makes: 4 Servings

INGREDIENTS
1 Daikon Radish, spiralized
1 lb. Ribeye Steak, sliced into strips
1 tablespoon Coconut Flour
1/2 teaspoon Guar Gum
1 tablespoon Coconut Oil
4 tablespoons Soy Sauce
1 teaspoon Sesame Oil
1 teaspoon Oyster Sauce
1 tablespoon + 1 teaspoon Rice Vinegar
1 teaspoon Sriracha or Sambal Olek and ½ teaspoon Red Pepper Flakes
1 tablespoon Toasted Sesame Seeds
1 bell pepper, sliced into thin strips
1 Jalapeno Pepper, sliced into thin rings
1 Green Onion, chopped
1 clove of Garlic, minced
1 teaspoon Ginger, minced
7 drops of Liquid Stevia Oil for frying

DIRECTIONS
In a bowl, toss the rib eye steak with coconut flour and guar gum. Heat the coconut oil and add the garlic, ginger, and red pepper strips for 2 minutes, or until fragrant. Add Soy sauce, oyster sauce, sesame oil, rice vinegar, stevia, and sriracha for 1 minute. After that, toss the sesame seeds and red pepper flakes into the sauce mixture.

Heat frying oil in a saucepan or fryer over high heat and add the beef strips; fry for 3 minutes on each side. After that, add the crispy meat to the wok pan with the sauce and toss to blend. Cook for a further 2 minutes. Drain and divide the daikon radish noodles among serving dishes. Serve with a portion of sesame beef on top of each. Serve with jalapeño slices and green onion as garnish.

412 calories, 33g Fats, 5g Carbohydrates, and 25g Protein.

46. Velveeta and Ground Beef Dinner

Total Prep Time: 10 Minutes | Total Cook Time: 25 Minutes| Makes: 6 Servings

INGREDIENTS
1 lb. lean ground beef
1 tablespoon onion powder
8 oz. Velveeta cheese, cubed
salt, and pepper
1/4 cup low-fat milk
1 lb. egg noodles, cooked
1 tablespoon chopped garlic
1 tablespoon Worcestershire sauce

DIRECTIONS
Heat a skillet and cook the beef until browned completely. Stir in the onion powder, salt, and black pepper. Meanwhile, in another pan, add the Velveeta cheese cubes. Stir in the milk, Worcestershire sauce, garlic, onion powder, salt, and pepper, and cook, stirring continuously till smooth. In the pan of beef, add the Velveeta sauce and noodles and stir to combine. Serve immediately.

Calories 522.5, Fat 17.0g, Cholesterol 79.8mg, Sodium 648.3mg, Carbohydrates 62.8g, Protein 32.8g

47. Bacon Cheeseburger Casserole

Total Prep Time: 10 Minutes| Total Cook Time: 45 Minutes| Makes: 6 Servings

INGREDIENTS
1 lb. Ground Beef
3 slices Bacon
1/2 cup Almond Flour
265g Cauliflower, riced
1 tablespoon Psyllium Husk Powder
1/2 teaspoon Garlic Powder
1/2 teaspoon Onion Powder
2 tablespoons Reduced Sugar Ketchup
1 tablespoon Dijon Mustard
2 tablespoons Mayonnaise
3 Eggs
4 oz. Cheddar Cheese, shredded
Salt and Pepper to Taste

DIRECTIONS
Pre-heat oven to 350F. In a food processor, rice the cauliflower. Combine the dry ingredients in a mixing bowl. In a food processor, combine bacon and ground beef until crumbly and slightly pasty. Season with salt and pepper to taste and cook. In a mixing bowl, combine all of the ingredients plus half of the cheddar cheese. Combine the eggs, mayonnaise, and ketchup in a mixing bowl. Fill a baking pan with the mixture and line it with parchment paper. Then sprinkle cheddar cheese on top. Bake for 40 minutes.

Calories 478, Fat 8.0g, Cholesterol 79.8mg, Sodium 648.3mg, Carbohydrates 62.8g, Protein 35g

48. Slow Cooker Braised Oxtails

Total Prep Time: 10 Minutes| Total Cook Time: 10 Minutes| Makes: 3 Servings

INGREDIENTS
2 lbs. Oxtails (Bone-in)
2 cups Beef Broth
1/3 cup butter
2 tablespoons Soy Sauce
1 tablespoon Fish Sauce
3 tablespoons Tomato Paste
1 teaspoon Onion Powder
1 teaspoon Minced Garlic
1/2 teaspoon Ground Ginger
1 teaspoon Dried Thyme
Salt and Pepper to Taste
1/2 teaspoon Guar Gum

DIRECTIONS
Combine the beef broth, soy sauce, fish sauce, tomato paste, and butter in a mixing bowl. Add the oxtails to the slow cooker as well.
Onion powder, chopped garlic, ground ginger, dried thyme, and salt and pepper to taste Season the oxtails and broth.
That concludes our discussion. Put it in your calendar and forget about it: Cook for 7 hours on low.
Remove the oxtail from the slow cooker and set it aside to drain on paper towels.
Blend the residual fluids in the slow cooker with an immersion blender. To achieve a cohesive and thicker gravy, add Guar Gum while blending.

433 Calories, 27g Fats, 2g Carbohydrates, and 23g Protein.

49. Perfect Ribeye Steak

Total Prep Time: 10 Minutes| Total Cook Time: 14 Minutes| Makes: 2 Servings

INGREDIENTS
1 tablespoons Butter
1 teaspoon Thyme, chopped
16 oz. Ribeye Steak
1 tablespoon Duck Fat
Salt and Pepper to Taste

DIRECTIONS
Rub your steak with a little layer of duck fat or oil to prepare it. Then season generously, with salt and pepper. Place your steak in a cast-iron pan with the duck fat or oil and sear it. After flipping the steak, place it in the oven for 6 minutes. Remove the steak from the oven and set it over low heat on the stovetop. In the same pan, melt the butter and add the thyme. Use it to coat the steak. Scoop the butter up with a spoon and ladle it over the steak by pushing the cast iron's handle downward. Cover with foil or a lid and set aside for 5 minutes.

740 Calories, 66g Fats, 0g Carbohydrates, 39g Protein.

50. Mediterranean Moroccan Meatballs

Total Prep Time: 10 Minutes| Total Cook Time: 20 Minutes| Makes: 4 Servings

INGREDIENTS
1 lb. Ground Lamb
1 tablespoon Finely Chopped Fresh Mint
1 tablespoon Finely Chopped Fresh Cilantro
2 teaspoon Fresh Thyme
1 teaspoon Minced Garlic
1 teaspoon Ground Coriander
1 teaspoon Kosher Salt
1 teaspoon Ground Cumin
1/2 teaspoon Onion Powder
1/2 teaspoon Allspice
1/4 teaspoon Paprika
1/4 teaspoon Oregano
1/4 teaspoon Curry Powder
1/4 teaspoon Black Pepper
Faux Yogurt Sauce
1/2 cup Coconut Cream
2 tablespoons Coconut Water
1 1/4 teaspoon Cumin
1 tablespoon Finely Chopped Fresh Cilantro
Zest 1/2 Lemon
1 teaspoon Lemon Juice

DIRECTIONS
Preheat the oven to 350 degrees Fahrenheit. Add the chopped spices, garlic, coriander, salt, cumin, onion powder, allspice, paprika, oregano, curry powder, and black pepper to the ground lamb. Make 18 meatballs out of the meat. Bake the meatballs for 15 minutes, or until the center is no longer pink. Add the coconut water, cumin, cilantro, and/or mint. Mix thoroughly and then add the zest and lemon juice. Mix thoroughly.

399 Calories, 35g Fats, 3g Carbohydrates, and 15g Protein.

51. Saucy Beef Skillet

Total Prep Time: 5 Minutes| Total Cook Time: 45 Minutes| Makes: 6 Servings

INGREDIENTS
500 g minced beef
1 tablespoon beef stock, dried instant
4 tablespoons olive oil
2 bay leaves
1 onion, finely diced
Worcestershire sauce, dash
2 garlic cloves, peeled and crushed
1 teaspoon allspice
1 teaspoon cinnamon
1 teaspoon paprika
130 g tomato paste
500 g pasta sauce

DIRECTIONS
Preheat a skillet over high heat.
In it, heat the oil. Cook for 6 minutes after adding the onion, garlic, meat, and spices.
Cook for 30 minutes on low heat, stirring often, after adding the tomato and pasta sauce, paprika, beef stock, bay leaves, salt, and pepper.
Serve your juicy meat with spaghetti while it's still hot.

Calories 361.1, Fat 24 g, Cholesterol 58.3 mg, Sodium, 578.8 mg, Carbohydrates 18.4 g, Protein 18.3 g

52. Cheeseburger Muffins

Total Prep Time: 10 Minutes| Total Cook Time: 20 Minutes| Makes: 9 Servings

INGREDIENTS
1/4 teaspoon Pepper
1/2 cup Blanched Almond Flour
1/2 cup Flaxseed Meal
1 teaspoon Baking Powder
1/2 teaspoon salt
2 Eggs
1/4 cup Sour Cream
FILLING
2 tablespoons Tomato Paste
16 oz. Ground Beef
1/2 teaspoon Onion Powder
1/2 teaspoon Garlic Powder
Salt and Pepper to Taste
TOPPINGS
2 tablespoons Reduced Sugar Ketchup
1/2 cup Cheddar Cheese
18 slices of Baby Dill Pickles
2 tablespoons Mustard

DIRECTIONS
Season beef with onion powder, garlic powder, salt, pepper, and tomato paste and lightly brown it on a hot skillet. Remove the pan from the heat and stir in the remaining ingredients. Preheat the oven to 350 degrees Fahrenheit and combine the dry ingredients for the muffins.
Mix the wet ingredients into the dry ingredients thoroughly. Fill silicone muffin cups halfway with the muffin batter. To make room for the ground beef, indent the muffin with your finger or a spoon. Fill each muffin halfway with the ground beef mixture. Bake for 15 minutes, or until the outsides of the muffins are gently browned. Remove from the oven, sprinkle with cheese, and broil for another 3 minutes.
Serve and top with diced pickles or mustard.

246 Calories, 16g Fats, 9g Carbohydrates, and 12g Protein.

53. Italian Stuffed Meatballs

Total Prep Time: 10 Minutes| Total Cook Time: 20 Minutes| Makes: 4 Servings

INGREDIENTS
1 1/2 lb. Ground Beef (80/20)
1 teaspoon Oregano
1/2 teaspoon Italian Seasoning
2 teaspoon Minced Garlic
1/2 teaspoon Onion powder
3 tablespoons Tomato Paste
3 tablespoons Flaxseed Meal
2 Eggs
1/2 cup Olives, sliced
1/2 cup Mozzarella Cheese
1 teaspoon Worcestershire
Sauce
Salt and Pepper to Taste

DIRECTIONS
Combine the ground beef, oregano, Italian seasoning, garlic, and onion powder in a mixing bowl. Using your hands, combine the ingredients.
Remix the meat with eggs, tomato paste, flaxseed, and Worcestershire sauce.
Finally, chop your olives into little pieces and combine them with the shredded mozzarella cheese in your meat. Everything should be mixed.
Preheat the oven to 400 degrees Fahrenheit and begin forming the meatballs. In total, you'll have roughly 20 meatballs. Place on a foil-lined cookie sheet.
Bake the meatballs in the oven for 18 minutes, or until done to your liking.
Serve with a simple spinach salad on the side and a drizzle of the cookie sheet grease.

594 Calories, 48g Fats, 8g Carbohydrates, and 38g Protein

54. Tater Tot Nachos

Total Prep Time: 10 Minutes| Total Cook Time: 5 Minutes| Makes: 3 Servings

INGREDIENTS
2 servings Tater Tots
6 oz. Ground Beef (80/20), cooked
2 oz. Cheddar Cheese, shredded
2 tablespoons Sour Cream
6 Black Olives, sliced
1 tablespoons Salsa
1/2 Jalapeno Pepper, sliced

DIRECTIONS
Place 10 tater tots in a casserole dish followed by ground beef and shredded cheese.
Build the second layer with the remaining tater tots.
Broil for 5 minutes to melt the cheese.
Serve with salsa, jalapenos, sour cream, and black olives.

637 Calories, 55g Fats, 5g Carbohydrates, and 33g of Protein.

55. Pulled Pork Sandwiches

Total Prep Time: 10 Minutes| Total Cook Time: 25 Minutes| Makes: 3 Servings

INGREDIENTS
1/2 lb. fresh lean pork, shredded
1/4 cup Barbecue sauce
2 tablespoons Olive oil
1 teaspoon Sea salt
2 cloves Garlic, minced
1 teaspoon Cayenne pepper
6 slices Bread

DIRECTIONS

Preheat your electric cooker to 400 degrees Fahrenheit. Drizzle half of the olive oil over the pork, then toss with the salt and garlic until thoroughly covered. Roast for about 20 minutes, or until slightly crispy and browned. Add the remaining tablespoon of olive oil to a skillet and cook. Combine the pork and barbecue sauce in a pan. Cook the pork in the sauce, stirring constantly, for 5 minutes, or until the sauce is fragrant and heated. Top bread slices with this mixture.

Calories: 490, Carbs: 61g, Fat: 11g

56. Cheese Stuffed Bacon Burger

Total Prep Time: 10 Minutes| Total Cook Time: 10 Minutes| Makes: 2 Servings

INGREDIENTS
8 oz. Ground Beef
2 slices Bacon, pre-cooked
1 oz. Mozzarella Cheese
2 oz. Cheddar Cheese
1 teaspoon salt
1/2 teaspoon Pepper
1 teaspoon Cajun Seasoning
1 tablespoons Butter

DIRECTIONS
Combine all of the spices in a mixing bowl and toss lightly. Cubed 1 oz. Mozzarella and sliced 2 oz. Cheddar is used to make the cheese. Make rough patties out of the ground beef and stuff them with mozzarella, enveloping the cheese with the beef. In a pan, melt 1 tablespoon of butter until it is sizzling and hot. Place the burger in the pan. Allow cooking for 3 minutes under a cloche. Place cheddar cheese on top of the burger after flipping it.
Replace the cloche over the top and continue to simmer for another 2 minutes, or until the desired temperature is attained. Half a bacon slice and arrange it on top of the burger.

614 Calories, 51g Fats, 5g Carbohydrates, and 33g Protein.

57. Pigs in a Blanket

Total Prep Time: 10 Minutes| Total Cook Time: 40 Minutes| Makes: 6 Servings

INGREDIENTS
37 Smokies
8 oz. Cheddar Cheese, melted
3/4 cup Almond Flour
1 tablespoon Psyllium Husk Powder
5 oz. Cream Cheese
1 Egg
1/2 teaspoon salt
1/2 teaspoon Pepper

DIRECTIONS
To prepare the dough, combine all of the ingredients. Spread the dough out on a Silpat sheet until it is completely covered. Check to see if it's even.
Refrigerate the dough for 20 minutes to solidify. While you're doing this, preheat your oven to 400 degrees Fahrenheit.
Transfer the dough on foil to cut once it has cooled.
Cut the dough into strips and wrap the Little Smokies in them. After that, bake for another 15 minutes. You may also broil them for 2 minutes before pulling them out.
Serve when still hot. It would be ideal if the sauce was tangy and slightly sweet.

72 Calories, 9g Fats, 0.6g Carbohydrates, and 8g Protein.

58. BBQ Bacon-Wrapped Smokies

Total Prep Time: 10 Minutes| Total Cook Time: 35 Minutes| Makes: 4 Servings

INGREDIENTS
24 small smokies
6 slices of bacon, chopped
3 tablespoons BBQ Sauce
Salt and Pepper to taste

DIRECTIONS
Preheat the oven to 375 degrees Fahrenheit. Place a smokie on top of the bacon slice. Roll up the mini smokie in the bacon. Insert a toothpick into the overlapping piece and place it on a foil-lined cookie sheet. Bake the smokies for 25 minutes after repeating the process with the remaining smokies. Remove the smokies from the oven and coat them with BBQ sauce using a basting brush. They should be thoroughly coated. Return to the oven for another 10 minutes of baking. Remove from the oven and set aside to cool for a few minutes. Parmesan cheese and chopped spring onion are sprinkled on top.

329 Calories, 25g Fats, 2g Carbohydrates, and 15g Protein.

59. Sirloin Onion Egg Noodles

Total Prep Time: 10 Minutes| Total Cook Time: 6 Hours| Makes: 8 Servings

INGREDIENTS
2 lb. sirloin tips, cubed
1/2 cup red wine
1 onion, chopped
1.25 oz. package beef with onion soup
20 oz. condensed mushroom soup cream
32 oz. egg noodles
1 cup milk

DIRECTIONS
Stir fry the meat and onion for about 5 minutes in a skillet.
Meanwhile, combine the mushroom soup, wine, milk, and soup mix in a mixing dish.
Pour the mixture into the skillet and bring to a low boil.
Reduce heat to low and cook for about 2 hours, covered.
Lower the heat to the lowest level and cook for about 4 hours, covered.
Cook the egg noodles for 5 minutes in a big pot of lightly salted boiling water.
Drain thoroughly.
To serve, spoon the meat mixture over the noodles.

Calories 684 kcal, Fat 16.9 g, Carbohydrates 90.6g, Protein 38.2 g, Cholesterol 146 mg, Sodium 902

60. Stuffed Pork Tenderloin & Radish

Total Prep Time: 10 Minutes| Total Cook Time: 1 Hour| Makes: 5 Servings

INGREDIENTS
PORK
2 lb. Pork Tenderloin, butterflied
3 teaspoon Kosher Salt
1 teaspoon Pepper
1 1/2 teaspoon Onion Powder
1 teaspoon Garlic Powder
2 teaspoons thyme
2 teaspoons Rosemary
1 lb. Ground Pork Sausage
3 oz. Baby Bella Mushrooms
3 oz. Spinach
1/2 teaspoon thyme
1/2 teaspoon Rosemary
1/4 teaspoon Garlic Powder
1/4 teaspoon Onion Powder
Salt and Pepper to Taste
RADISH
16 oz. Red Radish
4 tablespoons Duck Fat
1 teaspoon Rosemary
Salt and Pepper to Taste

DIRECTIONS
Season the pork with salt, pepper, onion powder, garlic powder, thyme, and rosemary on both sides.
Start frying the sausage in a pan while breaking up the sausage with a spatula once it begins to brown, then add the mushrooms, salt, pepper, onion powder, garlic powder, thyme, rosemary, and any other seasonings you desire.
Add the spinach.
Pour the mixture over the tenderloin and properly distribute it.
Roll it up using a butcher netting.
Cook this at 400F for 1 hour.
Meanwhile, cut all of your radishes in half and combine them with duck fat, salt, pepper, and rosemary.
Serve.

678 Calories, 46g Fats, 2g Carbohydrates, and 52g Protein.

61. Roasted Lemon Herb Chicken

Total Prep Time: 10 Minutes| Total Cook Time: 1 Hour | Makes: 4 Servings

INGREDIENTS:
12 pieces of bone-in chicken thighs & legs
1 teaspoon dried thyme
1 orange, sliced thin
1 medium onion, thinly sliced
1 tablespoon dried rosemary
1 lemon, sliced thin
FOR THE MARINADE:
Juice of 1 lemon
3 tablespoons extra virgin olive oil
3 cloves of garlic, minced
2 drops of stevia
Pinch low sodium salt and freshly ground pepper
1 teaspoon onion powder
1 tablespoon Italian seasoning
Juice of 1 orange
Dash of red pepper flakes

DIRECTIONS:
Mix all of the marinade ingredients. Place the chicken in a baking dish and pour the marinade over it. In a baking dish, arrange the onion, orange, and lemon slices on top of the chicken. Season to taste with thyme, rosemary, low sodium salt, and pepper. Cover with aluminum foil and bake for 30 minutes. Remove the foil, baste the chicken, and bake for another 30 minutes.

Calories: 405.3|Protein: 32.2g |Carbohydrates: 3.6g |Dietary Fiber: 1.5g |Sugars: 0.1g|Fat: 29.2g |Saturated Fat: 7.8g |Cholesterol: 127.7mg|Iron: 2mg |Sodium: 177.6mg

62. Basil Turkey with Roasted Tomatoes

Total Prep Time: 10 Minutes| Total Cook Time: 1 Hour | Makes: 4 Servings

INGREDIENTS:
1/2 cup thinly sliced fresh basil
2 turkey breasts
a few drops of stevia
1 cup mushrooms, chopped
1/2 medium onion, chopped
Fresh parsley, for garnish
1-2 tablespoons extra virgin olive oil
1-pint cherry tomatoes
Pinch low sodium salt and pepper

DIRECTIONS:
Drizzle olive oil and stevia over the tomatoes on a baking sheet. Add salt and pepper. Bake until soft, about 20 minutes. In a big pan, heat one tablespoon of olive oil over low heat. Cook for 10 minutes to soften the onions and mushrooms. Place the turkey in the pan after seasoning it with low sodium salt and pepper. Cook for 15 minutes, or until the chicken is fully cooked. Arrange the tomatoes on two dishes. Place one turkey breast on each plate, followed by the onions, mushrooms, and pan drippings. Serve with parsley as a garnish.

Calories 300|Total Fat 14 g|Saturated Fat 6 g |Cholesterol 100 mg |Sodium 480 mg |Total Carbohydrate 23 g|Dietary Fiber 2 g |Sugars 3 g| Protein 26 g

63. Turkey Squash Scramble

Total Prep Time: 10 Minutes| Total Cook Time: 10 Minutes | Makes: 4 Servings

INGREDIENTS:
2 bell peppers
1 teaspoon cumin
1 teaspoon chili powder
1-pound ground turkey
1 teaspoon garlic powder
1 teaspoon low sodium salt
1 tablespoon fresh cilantro
2 squash
2 onions
1 handful of spinach

DIRECTIONS:
Brown the turkey in a large skillet.
Mix in the thinly sliced onions, peppers, and squash/zucchini until they soften.
Add the fresh spinach to the pan with the turkey.
Cook until the spinach has wilted, seasoning with salt and pepper.
Remove from the pan and top with whatever toppings you choose.

Calories 260 |Total Fat 5 g|Saturated Fat 1 g |Cholesterol 45 mg|Sodium 610 mg |Total Carbohydrate 32 g |Dietary Fiber 9 g |Sugars 9 g|Protein 24 g

64. Spicy Turkey Stir Fry

Total Prep Time: 10 Minutes| Total Cook Time: 34 Minutes| Makes: 3 Servings

INGREDIENTS:
1 teaspoon garam masala
2 bell peppers, thinly sliced
2 lbs. boneless skinless turkey breasts, cut into 1-inch slices
2 tablespoons coconut oil
Pinch low sodium salt
2 teaspoons freshly ground pepper
1 teaspoon cumin seeds
FOR THE MARINADE:
1/2 cup coconut cream
1 teaspoon ginger, minced
1 clove of garlic, minced
1/4 teaspoon turmeric
1 teaspoon low sodium salt

DIRECTIONS:
Combine all of the marinade ingredients.
Add the chicken and marinate for at least 1 hour.
In a wok or large sauté pan, melt the coconut oil over medium-high heat, then add the cumin seeds and cook for 3 minutes.
After adding the marinated chicken/turkey, cook for 5 minutes. Until the chicken/turkey begins to brown, stir in the peppers, garam masala, and freshly ground pepper.
Add a pinch of low-sodium salt to taste.
Cook for 5 minutes, stirring regularly.

233 calories| 6g fat (1g saturated fat)|70mg cholesterol| 866mg sodium| 13g carbohydrate (0 sugars, 3g fiber)| 33g protein

65. Chicken Salad in Lettuce Cups

Total Prep Time: 10 Minutes | Makes: 6 Servings

INGREDIENTS:
1/4 cup plain, non-fat Greek yogurt
1/4 cup walnuts, roasted and chopped
2 boneless, skinless chicken breasts, boiled and shredded
Juice of 1 lemon
1/8 teaspoon black pepper
1/4 teaspoon, salt, divided
2 tablespoons cider vinegar
2 tablespoons olive oil
1/4 cup raisins
1 apple, diced
1 cup seedless red grapes, diced
12 leaves Bibb lettuce

DIRECTIONS:
In a large mixing bowl, combine the yogurt, olive oil, vinegar, lemon juice, pepper, and salt.
Toss the dressing with the shredded chicken, toasted walnuts, apple, grapes, celery, and raisins. Half-fill lettuce cups with chicken salad and serve.

350 Calories, 15g Fat (2g Saturated), 85mg Cholesterol, 237mg Sodium, 22g Carbohydrate (2g fiber, 16g Sugar, 0g Added), 34g Protein

66. Turkey Stuffed Boats

Total Prep Time: 10 Minutes| Total Cook Time: 30 Minutes | Makes: 6 Servings

INGREDIENTS:
1 tablespoon olive oil
2 tablespoons chopped parsley
4 zucchini
14-ounce can of diced tomatoes
8 ounces 93% lean ground turkey
4 cups spinach, chopped
1 onion, diced
2 cloves garlic, minced
1/4 cup panko breadcrumbs
1/4 teaspoon red pepper flakes
1/4 cup grated parmesan cheese

DIRECTIONS:
Cut the zucchini in half lengthwise and use a spoon to scrape out the seeds and flesh.
In a baking dish, arrange the zucchini halves. In a medium-sized skillet, heat the oil. Cook onions for 4 minutes, stirring occasionally. Add ground turkey, zucchini flesh, and garlic. Cook, stirring occasionally until the sauce has thickened somewhat. Add spinach and cook for a further 2 minutes, or until the spinach has wilted.
Combine breadcrumbs, parmesan, and parsley in a small bowl. Distribute the turkey and vegetable mixture evenly between the zucchini halves. Top with the breadcrumb mixture. Bake for 20 minutes, or until golden brown on top.

257 Calories, 8g Fat (2g Saturated), 33 mg Cholesterol, 190mg Sodium, 31g Carbohydrates (8g fiber, 15g Sugar, 0g Added), 21g Protein,

67. Taco Lettuce Cups

Total Prep Time: 10 Minutes| Total Cook Time: 14 Minutes | Makes: 6 Servings

INGREDIENTS:
8 ounces button mushrooms, diced
8 ounces 93% lean ground turkey
1 tablespoon olive oil
1/4 teaspoon cayenne
1 onion, diced
1 tablespoon cumin
2 teaspoons cornstarch
2 cloves garlic, minced
2 tablespoons ground chili
1/2 teaspoon salt
1 1/2 teaspoons paprika
12 leaves lettuce
2/3 cup water

DIRECTIONS:
In a large sauté pan, heat the oil over medium heat. Cook onions for 3 minutes.
Add turkey and cook for about 5 minutes, or until the ground turkey is no longer pink.
Add the diced mushrooms and simmer for a further 3 minutes.
Combine chili powder, cumin, cornstarch, paprika, salt, and cayenne pepper in a small bowl.
Add the spice mixture and water to the pan once the mushrooms have softened, and bring to a simmer for another 2 minutes.

Calories: 405.3|Protein: 32.2g |Carbohydrates: 3.6g |Dietary Fiber: 1.5g |Sugars: 0.1g|Fat: 29.2g |Saturated Fat: 7.8g |Cholesterol: 127.7mg|Iron: 2mg |Sodium: 177.6mg

68. Sunflower Seed Pesto Chicken

Total Prep Time: 10 Minutes| Total Cook Time: 20 Minutes | Makes: 4 Servings

INGREDIENTS:
PESTO
1 clove of garlic, chopped
2 tablespoons raw, hulled sunflower seeds
1 cup basil leaves
1/4 cup olive oil
1/8 teaspoon black pepper
2 tablespoons grated parmesan cheese
1/8 teaspoon salt
CHICKEN AND GARNISHES
1/4 cup shredded part-skim mozzarella cheese, divided
2 boneless, skinless chicken breasts, sliced lengthwise
2 tomatoes, sliced

DIRECTIONS:
Place the chicken on a rimmed baking sheet that has been oiled. In a food processor, add all of the pesto ingredients and process until smooth. In a food processor, combine basil, sunflower seeds, parmesan cheese, garlic, salt, and pepper. To combine, pulse a couple of times. Drizzle in the oil while the machine is running until the sauce is smooth.
Top each piece of chicken with pesto, tomato slices, and mozzarella. Bake for 15 minutes, or until thoroughly cooked.

244 Calories, 10g Fat (2g Saturated), 47mg Cholesterol, 314mg Sodium, 19g Carbohydrates (8g fiber, 11g Sugar, 0g Added), 25g Protein

69. Hearty Cauliflower Rice with Chicken

Total Prep Time: 10 Minutes| Total Cook Time: 14 Minutes | Makes: 4 Servings

INGREDIENTS:
3/4 cup orange juice
3 tablespoons oil
1 1/2 tablespoons low-sodium soy sauce
1 head cauliflower
2 boneless, skinless chicken breasts, cubed
1 teaspoon fresh ginger, grated
1/4 teaspoon black pepper
1 teaspoon turmeric powder
2 tablespoons rice wine vinegar
1 tablespoon honey
1 tablespoon corn starch
1/2 red bell pepper, diced
1 cup frozen peas and carrots, mixed
2 large eggs, beaten
3 scallions, sliced, whites & greens divided
3 cloves garlic, minced

DIRECTIONS:
In a mixing bowl, combine orange juice, rice wine vinegar, soy sauce, honey, cornstarch, and ginger. Before adding the eggs and black pepper, coat the pan with cooking spray. Scramble the eggs well. Toss in the peas and carrots, scallion, garlic, and bell pepper with the remaining tablespoon of oil in the skillet. Cook for 4 minutes, or until the veggies are cooked, stirring regularly. Toss in the riced cauliflower, coated with cooking spray. Cook for another 5 minutes, stirring regularly, or until cauliflower is somewhat crunchy. In a skillet with the cauliflower, sauté the cooked chicken, eggs, veggies, and sauce until the sauce thickens, about 3 minutes. Remove the pan from the heat and top with scallion greens.

132 Calories, 3g Fat (1g Saturated), 90mg Cholesterol, 223mg Sodium, 14g Carbohydrates (3g fiber, 8g Sugar), 15g Protein

70. Creamy Baked Chicken

Total Prep Time: 10 Minutes| Total Cook Time: 12 Minutes | Makes: 4 Servings

INGREDIENTS:
1 tablespoon olive oil
1/2 cup shredded low-fat cheddar cheese
2 medium boneless, skinless chicken breasts, sliced lengthways
1 teaspoon black pepper
1/3 cup Greek yogurt
1 teaspoon onion powder
1/2 cup panko
1 teaspoon garlic powder

DIRECTIONS:
Arrange your chicken on a well-oiled rimmed baking sheet. Dredge with Greek yogurt. Combine panko, cheddar cheese, olive oil, garlic powder, onion powder, and black pepper in a small mixing bowl. Sprinkle this mixture on top of the chicken and push it down. Bake the chicken for 12 minutes at 425 degrees.

193 Calories, 7g Fat (2g Saturated), 39mg Cholesterol, 363mg Sodium, 12g Carbohydrates (1g fiber, 2g Sugar, 1g Added), 20g Protein

71. Sweet Potato Chicken Dumplings

Total Prep Time: 10 Minutes| Total Cook Time: 30 Minutes | Makes: 8 Servings

INGREDIENTS:
1 cup frozen peas
1 cup carrots, sliced
1 tablespoon olive oil
2 cloves garlic, minced
1 cup green beans, trimmed and halved
1 teaspoon baking soda
1 teaspoon black pepper, divided
1 onion, chopped
1 cup kale, stemmed and chopped
1 cup wheat flour
1/2 cup all-purpose flour, divided
1 cup buttermilk
3 cups cooked chicken breast, shredded
1 sweet potato, cooked, peeled, and mashed
2 cups low-sodium chicken broth
1/8 teaspoon salt

DIRECTIONS:
In a skillet, heat the oil.
Toss the sautéed onions with carrots, green beans, peas, kale, garlic, and pepper. Cook for 8 minutes, stirring occasionally. Cook for another 3 minutes after adding the flour. Toss the broth, vegetables, and flour mixture into a pot and bring to a boil. Toss the vegetables and shredded chicken together. Evenly distribute the batter among the 16 muffin cups. Combine the flours, baking soda, salt, and remaining pepper in a mixing basin. Mix in the mashed sweet potato and buttermilk. Divide the batter evenly among the 16 muffin cups, then top with the chicken mixture. Bake for 15 minutes, or until golden brown on top.

190 Calories, 4g Fat (1g Saturated), 18mg Cholesterol, 385mg Sodium, 29g Carbohydrates (5g fiber, 5g Sugar, 0g Added), 12g Protein

72. Creamy Baked Chicken

Total Prep Time: 10 Minutes| Total Cook Time: 12 Minutes | Makes: 4 Servings

INGREDIENTS:
1 tablespoon olive oil
1/2 cup shredded low-fat cheddar cheese
2 medium boneless, skinless chicken breasts, sliced lengthways
1 teaspoon black pepper
1/3 cup Greek yogurt
1 teaspoon onion powder
1/2 cup panko
1 teaspoon garlic powder

DIRECTIONS:
Arrange your chicken on a well-oiled rimmed baking sheet. Dredge with Greek yogurt. Combine panko, cheddar cheese, olive oil, garlic powder, onion powder, and black pepper in a small mixing bowl. Sprinkle this mixture on top of the chicken and push it down. Bake the chicken for 12 minutes at 425 degrees.

193 Calories, 7g Fat (2g Saturated), 39mg Cholesterol, 363mg Sodium, 12g Carbohydrates (1g fiber, 2g Sugar, 1g Added), 20g Protein

73. Seared Chicken & Tomatoes

Total Prep Time: 10 Minutes| Total Cook Time: 15 Minutes | Makes: 4 Servings

INGREDIENTS:
2 chicken breasts, cut lengthwise
3 cloves garlic, minced
1 cup quinoa
1 tablespoon dill
1 teaspoon black pepper
Juice of 1 lemon
1 tablespoon vegetable oil
1 bell pepper, diced
1 teaspoon salt
1 cucumber diced
1 cup cherry tomatoes, quartered
1 cup reduced-fat feta cheese, crumbled

DIRECTIONS:
In a small mixing bowl, combine the oil, garlic cloves, and basil leaves.Toss the chicken breasts in the marinade in a zip-lock bag. In a small saucepan, bring the balsamic vinegar and honey to a boil.

In a small mixing dish, combine chopped tomatoes, remaining 2 garlic cloves, and 1/4 cup basil leaves; set aside. In a large sauté pan, heat the remaining 1 tablespoon of olive oil over medium-high heat. Cook 2 chicken breasts at a time in the pan for 3 minutes on each side, or until light golden brown. Drizzle 1/4 cup tomato mixture and balsamic glaze over chicken breast halves.

294 Calories,10g Fat (2g Saturated), 84mg Cholesterol, 88mg Sodium, 16g Carbohydrates (2g fiber, 12g Sugar, 4g Added), 32g Protein

74. Sheet Pan Fajitas

Total Prep Time: 10 Minutes| Total Cook Time: 25 Minutes | Makes: 4 Servings

INGREDIENTS:
2 bell peppers, sliced into thin strips
2 boneless, skinless chicken breasts, sliced into thin strips
8 corn tortillas
2 tablespoons olive oil
1 onion, sliced
3 cloves garlic, minced
2 limes, divided
1 tablespoon chili powder
1/2 cup Greek yogurt
3/4 teaspoon paprika
1 teaspoon cayenne
1 teaspoon salt
1/2 tablespoon cumin

DIRECTIONS:
Lightly grease and cover a rimmed baking sheet with foil.
Drizzle olive oil over the sliced chicken, onions, peppers, and garlic on the baking sheet. Combine chili powder, cumin, cornstarch, paprika, salt, and cayenne pepper in a small bowl. Season both the chicken and the veggies with the spice combination. Bake the chicken and vegetables for 25 minutes at 425 degrees. Meanwhile, zest and juice a lime, then combine with Greek yogurt. Serve the fajitas with a side of Greek yogurt and lime wedges.

282 Calories, 7g Fat (1g Saturated), 43mg Cholesterol, 236mg Sodium, 33g Carbohydrates (6g fiber, 5g Sugar, 0g Added), 23g Protein

75. Chicken and Quinoa Soup

Total Prep Time: 10 Minutes| Total Cook Time: 20 Minutes | Makes: 6 Servings

INGREDIENTS:
1 onion, chopped
4 cups fat-free, low-sodium chicken broth
1 lb. boneless, skinless chicken breasts, cubed
1 cup water
3 large garlic cloves, minced
1 carrot, sliced
1 teaspoon pepper
1 tablespoon chopped, fresh thyme
1/2 cup uncooked quinoa
1 dried bay leaf
2 ounces sugar snap peas, sliced

DIRECTIONS
Mix the chicken, broth, onion, water, carrot, garlic, thyme, bay leaf, and pepper in a large pot. Bring to a boil. Reduce the heat to low and cook for 5 minutes, slightly covered. Stir in the quinoa thoroughly. Bake for 5 minutes at 350°F. Stir in the peas thoroughly. Cook, stirring occasionally, for 8 minutes, or until the quinoa is cooked. Remove the bay leaf before serving the soup.

Calories: 154, Total Fat: 2.5 g (Saturated Fat: .5 g, Unsaturated Fat: 1 g), Cholesterol: 48 Mg Sodium: 139 Mg, Total Carbohydrate: 12 g (Dietary Fiber: 2 g, Sugar: 3 g), Protein: 20 g

76. Chicken Cauliflower Casserole

Total Prep Time: 15 Minutes| Total Cook Time: 1 Hour 15 Minutes | Makes: 10 Servings

INGREDIENTS:
3 carrots, peeled and sliced
2 tablespoons coconut oil
2-2½ pounds bone-in chicken thighs and drumsticks
Salt and ground black pepper
1 onion, diced
2 garlic cloves, crushed
2 tablespoons fresh ginger root, chopped
1 teaspoon coriander powder
1 teaspoon ground cinnamon
½ teaspoon ground turmeric
1 teaspoon paprika
2 teaspoons cumin powder
¼ teaspoon cayenne pepper
28-ounce can of tomatoes with liquid
1 teaspoon of salt
1 head cauliflower, shredded
1 bell pepper, sliced
1 lemon, thinly sliced
Fresh parsley, crumbled

DIRECTIONS:
Preheat your oven to 375°F. Melt 1 tablespoon coconut oil. Add chicken and cook for 5 minutes on each side. In the same skillet, sauté the carrot, onion, garlic, and ginger over high heat for about 4-5 minutes. Add the spices and remaining coconut oil and stir. Add the chicken, tomatoes, peppers, parsley, and salt and simmer for about 3-5 minutes. Layer the cauliflower rice on the bottom of a rectangular baking dish. Spoon chicken mixture evenly over cauliflower rice and garnish with lemon wedges.
Bake for 1 hour.

Calories: 265| Fat: 16.8g | Carbs: 11.4g | Fiber: 4.2g | Sugars: 4.9g | Protein: 20g

77. Prawn Mexicana

Total Prep Time: 10 Minutes| Total Cook Time: 10 Minutes | Makes: 4 Servings

INGREDIENTS:
1 avocado, pitted and diced
2 tablespoons olive oil
1 lb. medium shrimp, peeled and deveined
Shredded lettuce, for serving
1 teaspoon low sodium salt
1 teaspoon chili powder
Fresh cilantro, for serving
1 lime, cut into wedges
FOR THE TORTILLAS:
1/2 teaspoon cumin
1/4 cup almond milk
6 egg whites
1/4 cup coconut flour
1 teaspoon low sodium salt
1/4 teaspoon chili powder

DIRECTIONS:
In a small mixing bowl, combine all of the tortilla ingredients and stir thoroughly. Preheat a skillet over medium-high heat. Toss the shrimp with olive oil, chile powder, and reduced-sodium salt to coat. Cook for about a minute per side in a skillet. Pour a little batter into the skillet. Cook for 2 minutes, scraping the sides with a spatula to loosen them up. When the bottom has firmed up, carefully flip it over and cook for another 3 minutes, or until lightly browned, before setting it aside on a dish. Place cooked shrimp, shredded lettuce, avocado, and cilantro on top of each tortilla. Serve with a wedge of lime.

Calories 10 |Total Fat 0.3g grams Saturated Fat 0.1g grams | Trans Fat 0g grams | Carbohydrates 0.5g grams | Dietary Fiber 0.1g grams | Sugars 0.1g grams | Protein 1,3g

78. Salmon with Lemon and Thyme

Total Prep Time: 10 Minutes| Total Cook Time: 25 Minutes | Makes: 4 Servings

INGREDIENTS:
1 tablespoons capers
32 oz. piece of salmon or any fresh white fish
1 lemon, sliced thin
low sodium salt and freshly ground pepper
1 tablespoon fresh thyme
Olive oil

DIRECTIONS:
Line a rimmed baking sheet with parchment paper and set the salmon on the prepared baking sheet, skin side down.
Season the salmon with salt and pepper that is low in sodium.
Capers, sliced lemon and thyme should be arranged on top of the salmon. Bake for 25 minutes.

Calories 329.1 | Total Fat 17.7g | Saturated fat 2.6g | Polyunsaturated fat 5.6 | Cholesterol 109.1mg | Sodium 126.5mg | Potassium 987.2mg | Carbohydrates 1g | Sugar 0g | Fiber 0.4g | Protein 39.5g

79. Shrimp Scampi in Spaghetti Sauce

Total Prep Time: 10 Minutes| Total Cook Time: 1 Hour | Makes: 4 Servings

INGREDIENTS:
FOR THE SPAGHETTI:
1 teaspoon dried oregano
1 spaghetti squash, cut in half
2 teaspoons dried basil
Pinch salt and pepper
FOR THE SHRIMP SCAMPI:
10 oz. shrimp, peeled and
deveined
2 tablespoons butter
3 cloves garlic, minced
Juice of 1 lemon
2 tablespoons olive oil
Pinch of red pepper flakes
1 tablespoon fresh parsley,
chopped
Pinch salt and pepper

DIRECTIONS:
Microwave the squash for 4 minutes to soften it.
Place the squash halves on a baking sheet.
Season with salt and pepper.
Roast for 50 minutes, or until the squash is fork-tender.
Scrape the squash to shred it into threads.
Melt the butter and olive oil in a skillet over medium heat after removing the spaghetti squash from the oven.
Add garlic, shrimp, reduced-sodium salt, pepper, and a pinch of red pepper flakes and cook for 5 minutes, or until the shrimp are fully cooked.
Remove from heat and stir in the cooked spaghetti squash to taste.
Toss with lemon zest and juice.
Garnish with parsley.

Calories: 363kcal | Carbohydrates: 46g | Protein: 11g | Fat: 13g | Saturated Fat: 4g | Cholesterol: 52mg | Sodium: 172mg | Potassium: 200mg | Fiber: 2g | Sugar: 2g | Vitamin A: 255IU | Vitamin C: 9.2mg | Calcium: 43mg | Iron: 1.3mg

80. Cod in Delish Sauce

Total Prep Time: 10 Minutes| Total Cook Time: 12 Minutes | Makes: 6 Servings

INGREDIENTS:
3 tablespoons extra virgin olive oil
3 tablespoons fresh parsley, chopped
1/3 cup almond flour
1/2 teaspoon low sodium salt
3 tablespoons lemon juice
1 lb. cod fillets
2 tablespoons walnut oil, divided
1 cup low sodium chicken stock
1/3 cup capers, drained

DIRECTIONS:
In a bowl, combine the almond flour and reduced-sodium salt.
Dredge the fish in the almond flour mixture.
In a skillet, heat enough olive oil to cover the bottom and one tablespoon of walnut oil over medium-high heat.
Add the fish to the pan and brown for 4 minutes per side.
Scrape any browned bits from the bottom of the skillet and add the chicken stock, lemon juice, and capers. Simmer.
Take the pan off the heat and add the remaining tablespoon of walnut oil. Divide the fish between dishes, pour with the sauce, and top with parsley.

Calories: 303kcal | Carbohydrates: 2g | Protein: 37g | Fat: 15g | Saturated Fat: 8g | Cholesterol: 112mg | Sodium: 455mg | Potassium: 769mg | Vitamin A: 970IU | Vitamin C: 11.6mg | Calcium: 244mg | Iron: 1.2mg

81. Salmon Fettuccini

Total Prep Time: 15 Minutes| Total Cook Time: 15 Minutes | Makes: 6 Servings

INGREDIENTS
12 ounces fresh salmon, cut into filets
Fresh basil
Sea salt and pepper to taste
1 tablespoon clarified butter
Juice one lemon, about 3 tablespoons
2 cloves garlic, minced
12 ounces spelt fettuccini, cooked
20 spinach leaves

DIRECTIONS
Preheat the grill.
Season the salmon fillet with salt & pepper to taste, then grill for 6 minutes, skin side down, before flipping.
Grill for 6 minutes more, or until the meat readily flakes off with a fork.
Heat lemon juice, and garlic with butter in a saucepan over medium heat.
Remove the skin from the salmon and cut it into flakes or chunks. Combine warm pasta, garlic-butter sauce, spinach, and fresh basil in a mixing bowl.

Calories 524| Fat 12g (Saturated 3g) | Cholesterol 62mg| Sodium 233mg| Carbohydrate 76g| Dietary Fiber 10g| Protein 35g.

82. Shrimp and Scallop Combo

Total Prep Time: 25 Minutes| Total Cook Time: 20 Minutes | Makes: 4-6 Servings

INGREDIENTS
1/2 cup chopped scallions
1 cup broccoli florets, steamed lightly
1 cup vegetable broth
4 tablespoons clarified butter, divided
1 clove of garlic, minced or pressed
1/2 cup green bell peppers, seeded and diced
1-pound shrimp, deveined
1-pound small bay scallops
3 tablespoons chopped basil
2 tablespoons chopped parsley
1 teaspoon marjoram
1/2 cup soy milk
2 tablespoons spelt flour
2 cups tomatoes, diced
10 ounces cooked spelt pasta

DIRECTIONS
Sauté the garlic, onions, and green bell peppers in half of the butter.
Add the vegetable broth and cook until the broth has evaporated.
Drain pasta and set aside according to package guidelines.
Bring soy milk to a low boil in a small pot. Slowly add in the spelt flour, stirring constantly until the mixture thickens. Remove from heat and stir.
Cook the shrimp, scallops, basil, parsley, and marjoram in the remaining butter for 3 minutes, uncovered.
Toss all ingredients with cooked pasta and serve immediately.

Calories 668| Fat 18g (Saturated 8g) | Cholesterol 257mg| Sodium 602mg| Carbohydrate 75g| Dietary Fiber 11g| Protein 56g.

83. Orange Poached Salmon

Total Prep Time: 15 Minutes| Total Cook Time: 15 Minutes | Makes: 3 Servings

INGREDIENTS:
1/2 cup fresh orange juice
4 garlic cloves, crushed
1 teaspoon fresh ginger, finely grated
3 tablespoons coconut aminos
3 salmon fillets

DIRECTIONS:
In a mixing bowl, combine all of the ingredients except the salmon fillets.
In the bottom of a skillet, place the salmon fillets.
Spread the ginger mixture evenly over the salmon and bring to a boil in a saucepan over high heat.
Reduce to low heat and cook, covered, for 9 minutes, or until the desired doneness is reached.

Calories: 259| Fat: 10.6g | Carbs: 7.3g | Fiber: 0.2g| Sugars: 2.4g | Protein: 33.4g

84. Paprika Salmon

Total Prep Time: 10 Minutes| Total Cook Time: 8 Minutes | Makes: 6 Servings

INGREDIENTS:
½ tablespoon ground ginger
½ tablespoon ground coriander
½ tablespoon ground cumin
½ teaspoon paprika
¼ teaspoon cayenne pepper
Pinch of salt
1 tablespoon of fresh orange juice
1 tablespoon coconut oil, melted
6 salmon fillets

DIRECTIONS:
Place all ingredients except salmon in a bowl and stir until paste forms.
Add the salmon and brush generously with the mixture.
Allow 30 minutes in the refrigerator to marinate.
For at least 10 minutes, preheat the gas grill on high.
Using cooking spray, coat the grill grate.
Grill salmon for a few minutes.
Cover with the lid and grill for about 4 minutes on each side.

Calories: 175| Fat: 9.5g| Carbohydrates: 1 g| Fiber: 0.2g| Sugars: 0.3 g| Protein: 22.2g

85. Honey Baked Salmon

Total Prep Time: 10 Minutes| Total Cook Time: 12 Minutes | Makes: 4 Servings

INGREDIENTS:
Pinch black pepper
2 salmon fillets
3 Tablespoons of raw honey
1/3 teaspoon ground turmeric
2 slices of lemon
2 salmon fillets

DIRECTIONS:
Place the salmon, ½ teaspoons honey, ¼ teaspoons turmeric, and black pepper in a Ziploc bag.
Close the bag and shake well.
Allow 1 hour in the refrigerator to marinate.
Preheat your oven to 40°F.
Transfer the salmon fillets to a baking sheet in a single layer.
Cover fillets with marinade.
Place the salmon fillets skin side up and bake for about 6 minutes on each side.
Sprinkle evenly with remaining turmeric and black pepper.
Place 1 slice of lemon on each fillet and drizzle with the remaining honey.
Cook for about 6 minutes.

Calories: 290| Fat: 10.5g | Carbs: 17.6g | Fiber: 0.1g| Sugars: 17.3g | Protein: 33.1g

86. Honey & Amino Glazed Salmon

Total Prep Time: 15 Minutes| Total Cook Time: 15 Minutes | Makes: 6 Servings

INGREDIENTS:
1 shallot, chopped
1 teaspoon garlic powder
¼ cup raw honey
1/3 cup fresh orange juice
1/3 cup coconut aminos
6 salmon fillets
1 teaspoon ginger powder

DIRECTIONS:
Put all the ingredients in a Ziploc bag and seal the bag.
Shake the bag to coat the salmon mixture.
Preheat grill to medium heat.
Remove the salmon from the marinade bag and set it aside.
Grill for about 15 minutes.

Calories: 216| Fat: 7.1g | Carbs: 16.5g | Fiber: 0.2g| Sugars: 12.9g | Protein: 22.3g

87. Black Pepper Salmon with Yogurt

Total Prep Time: 10 Minutes| Total Cook Time: 14 Minutes | Makes: 4 Servings

INGREDIENTS:
YOGURT MARINADE
¼ cup low-fat Greek yogurt
½ teaspoon ground coriander
½ teaspoon ground turmeric
½ teaspoon ground ginger
¼ teaspoon cayenne powder
Pinch Salt
Pinch ground black pepper
SALMON
4 skinless salmon fillets

DIRECTIONS:
Heat the broiler.
Place the salmon fillets in a single layer on the broiler pan.
Spoon the yogurt mixture evenly over each fillet.
Grill for about 15 minutes.

Calories: 313| Fat: 18.3g | Carbs: 1.4g | Fiber: 0.1g| Sugars: 1g | Protein: 34g

88. Crusted Salmon

Total Prep Time: 15 Minutes| Total Cook Time: 20 Minutes | Makes: 4 Servings

INGREDIENTS:
1 cup almonds
Pinch black pepper
1 tablespoon fresh dill, chopped
2 tablespoons fresh lemon zest, grated
½ teaspoons garlic salt
1 tablespoon olive oil
3-4 tablespoons Dijon mustard
4 salmon fillets
4 teaspoons fresh lemon juice

DIRECTIONS:
Pulse the nuts in a food processor until they are coarsely chopped.
Pulse the dill, lemon zest, garlic salt, black pepper, and butter into a crumbly mixture.
Arrange the salmon fillets on a lined baking sheet
Spread Dijon mustard on top of each salmon fillet.
Spread the nut mixture evenly over each fillet.
Bake for about 15 minutes.

Calories:350| Fat: 27.8g | Carbs: 5.2g | Fiber: 2.9g| Sugars: 0.8 g | Protein: 24.9g

89. Black Pepper Peach and Salmon

Total Prep Time: 15 Minutes| Total Cook Time: 12 Minutes | Makes: 4 Servings

INGREDIENTS:
4 salmon steaks
Pinch Salt
1 tablespoon balsamic vinegar
3 peaches, cored and quartered
1 tablespoon fresh ginger, chopped
1 teaspoon fresh thyme leaves, chopped
3 tablespoons of olive oil
Pinch ground black pepper

DIRECTIONS:
Preheat grill to medium heat.
Sprinkle salmon evenly with salt and black pepper.
In a mixing dish, combine the peach, salt, and black pepper.
Preheat the grill.
Place the peaches and salmon steaks on the grill for 5 minutes on each side.
Combine the remaining ingredients in a mixing bowl.
Spoon the ginger mixture evenly over the salmon fillets and serve with the peaches and onions.

Calories: 290| Fat: 17.9g | Carbs: 11.7g | Fiber: 2g | Sugars: 10.6g | Protein: 23.2g

90. Salmon with Spicy and Creamy Sauce

Total Prep Time: 15 Minutes| Total Cook Time: 35 Minutes | Makes: 5 Servings

INGREDIENTS:
5 salmon fillets
1½ teaspoons ground turmeric
Pinch of salt
3 tablespoons coconut oil
1 cinnamon stick, coarsely crushed
3-4 coarsely crushed green cardamom
4-5 whole cloves, coarsely crushed
2 bay leaves
1 onion, diced
1 teaspoon garlic paste
1½ teaspoons ginger paste
3-4 green chilies, halved
1 teaspoon red pepper powder
¾ cup plain Greek yogurt
¾ cup of water
¼ cup fresh cilantro, chopped

DIRECTIONS:
In a bowl, season the salmon with ½ teaspoon of turmeric and salt and set aside. In a skillet, melt 1 tablespoon of coconut oil and sear the salmon, for about 2 minutes on each side. Transfer the salmon to a bowl. In the same skillet, melt the remaining oil and sauté the cinnamon, green cardamom, whole cloves, and bay leaf for about 1 minute. Sauté for around 4 minutes after adding the onion, garlic paste, ginger paste, and green peppers. Reduce heat to medium-low.
Add the remaining turmeric, red chili powder, salt, and sauté for about 1 minute. Meanwhile, put the yogurt and water in a bowl and stir until smooth. Add the yogurt mixture, and simmer for about 15 minutes. Gently add the salmon fillets and simmer for about 5 minutes. Serve hot with cilantro.

Calories: 270| Fat: 16g | Carbs: 7.3g | Fiber: 1.4g| Sugars: 3.8g | Protein: 24.8g

91. Sumac Cod in Tomato Sauce

Total Prep Time: 15 Minutes| Total Cook Time: 35 Minutes | Makes: 5 Servings

INGREDIENTS:
1 teaspoon turmeric powder
1 onion, diced
8 garlic cloves, crushed
2 teaspoons sumac
2 jalapeño peppers, chopped
2 tablespoons lime juice
3 tablespoons of tomato paste
6 tomatoes, chopped
1 teaspoon ground cumin
5 cod fillets
2 tablespoons olive oil
2 teaspoons coriander
Pinch Salt
1 teaspoon dried dill weed
Pinch ground black pepper

DIRECTIONS:
Place the dill and spices in a bowl and mix well.
In a deep wok, heat the oil over high heat and sauté the onion for about 2 minutes.
Sauté for around 2 minutes with the garlic and jalapeno.
Stir in the tomatoes, tomato paste, lime juice, water, half the spice blend, salt, and pepper, and bring to a boil.
Cook, covered, for about 10 minutes over medium-low heat, stirring periodically.
Meanwhile, season the cod fillets evenly with the remaining spice blend, salt, and pepper.
Place the fish fillets in the wok and press lightly into the tomato mixture.
Cook, covered, for about 15 minutes.

Calories:301| Fat: 7.9g | Carbs: 12.2g | Fiber: 3g | Sugars: 5.9g | Protein: 45.2g

92. Mediterranean Ginger Tilapia

Total Prep Time: 10 Minutes| Total Cook Time: 6 Minutes | Makes: 5 Servings

INGREDIENTS:
3 tablespoons ginger, chopped
2 tablespoons coconut oil
2 tablespoons unsweetened coconut, grated
2 garlic cloves, crushed
2 tablespoons coconut aminos
5 tilapia fillets
8 spring onions, chopped

DIRECTIONS:
In a skillet, melt the coconut oil over and fry the tilapia fillets for about 2 minutes.
Toss in the garlic, coconut, and ginger and sauté for a minute on the other side.
Cook for 1 minute after adding the coconut aminos and the spring onion.

Calories: 266| Fat: 8.8g | Carbs: 19.9g | Fiber: 3.7g| Sugars: 1.5 g| Protein: 29.1g

93. Chard Haddock

Total Prep Time: 15 Minutes| Total Cook Time: 10 Minutes | Makes:1 Serving

INGREDIENTS:
2 tablespoons coconut oil
2 teaspoons fresh ginger, finely grated
1 fillet of haddock
2 garlic cloves, crushed
Salt and ground black pepper
2 cups Swiss chard, coarsely chopped
1 teaspoon coconut aminos

DIRECTIONS:
Sauté the garlic and ginger in cooking oil.
Add the haddock fillet with the salt and black pepper and cook for about 3 to 5 minutes on each side or until the desired doneness.
Meanwhile, in another saucepan, melt the remaining coconut oil over high heat and cook the chard and coconut aminos for about 5-10 minutes.
Serve the salmon fillet on the chard.

Calories: 402| Fat: 28.7g | Carbs: 8.2g | Fiber: 1.8g| Sugars: 1g | Protein: 29.5g

94. Citrus Snapper with Cilantro

Total Prep Time: 10 Minutes| Total Cook Time: 10 Minutes | Makes: 2 Servings

INGREDIENTS:
2 tablespoons coconut aminos
1 tablespoon fresh turmeric, grated
2 tablespoons garlic, minced
2 tablespoons olive oil
1 bunch of fresh cilantro, chopped
2 snapper fillets
2 tablespoons lime juice
1 tablespoon ginger, grated

DIRECTIONS:
Place the garlic, turmeric, ginger, lime juice, coconut aminos, and olive oil in a food processor and blend until smooth.
Pour the mixture into a bowl with the cilantro and mix well.
Add the snapper fillets and brush generously with the mixture.
Place each fish fillet in the center of a piece of aluminum foil.
Wrap the foil around the fish and secure it in place.
In a pot of boiling water, place a steamer basket.
Steam for about 8 minutes.

Calories: 390| Fat: 17.5g | Carbs: 10.1g | Fiber: 1.2g| Sugars: 0.3 g| Protein: 45.1g

95. Sea Bass with Vegetables

Total Prep Time: 15 Minutes| Total Cook Time: 15 Minutes | Makes: 2 Servings

INGREDIENTS:
1 sea bass fillet, diced
1 tablespoon coconut vinegar
¼ teaspoon ginger paste
¼ teaspoon garlic paste
1 teaspoon red pepper powder
1 tablespoon olive oil, extra-virgin
½ cup fresh button mushrooms, sliced
1 small onion, quartered
¼ cup red bell pepper, seeded and diced
Pinch of salt
¼ cup yellow bell peppers, seeded and diced
2-3 spring onions, chopped
1 teaspoon fish sauce

DIRECTIONS:
Combine fish, ginger, garlic, chili powder, and salt in a bowl and let sit for about 20 minutes.
In a nonstick skillet, heat 1 teaspoon of oil over high heat and sear the fish for about 3-4 minutes or until browned on all sides.
In another skillet, heat the remaining oil over high heat and sauté the mushrooms and onions, for about 5-7 minutes.
Sauté the peppers and salmon for around 2 minutes.
Toss in the spring onions and fish sauce and cook for about 3 minutes.

Calories: 280| Fat: 17.6g | Carbs: 8.8g | Fiber: 2.2g| Sugars: 3.8g | Protein: 23.9g

96. Citrusy Shrimp

Total Prep Time: 15 Minutes| Total Cook Time: 10 Minutes | Makes: 6 Servings

INGREDIENTS:
1 small onion, diced
1 tablespoon fresh ginger, chopped
1 tablespoon fresh lemon zest, finely grated
1 fresh red pepper, seeded and chopped
1 teaspoon ground turmeric
4 garlic cloves, crushed
½ cup olive oil
½ cup fresh lemon juice
20-24 raw shrimp, peeled and deveined
1 tablespoon coconut oil

DIRECTIONS:
Combine all ingredients in a large mixing bowl, except the shrimp and coconut oil.
Toss in the shrimp.
In a large nonstick skillet, melt the coconut oil over high heat and sauté the shrimp for 4 minutes.
Return the marinade to the pot and bring to a boil, stirring regularly.
Simmer for 1-2 minutes.

Calories: 268| Fat: 20.6g | Carbs: 4.2g | Fiber: 0.6g| Sugars: 1g | Protein: 17.2g

97. Pinto & Red Bean Chili

Total Prep Time: 10 Minutes| Total Cook Time: 55 Minutes | Makes: 4 Servings

INGREDIENTS
1 tablespoon olive oil
1 yellow onion, chopped
2 serrano chiles, seeded and minced
3 garlic cloves, minced
28-ounce can of crushed tomatoes
1 cup water
2 tablespoons chili powder
½ teaspoon dried marjoram
¼ teaspoon ground cayenne
Salt and freshly ground black pepper
1½ cups cooked pinto beans
3 cups cooked dark red kidney beans

DIRECTIONS
Heat the oil in a big saucepan over medium heat. Cook the onion, chiles, and garlic until they are softened, about 10 minutes.
Toss in the tomatoes, water, chili powder, marjoram, cayenne, and season with salt and pepper. Bring to a boil, then reduce to low heat, add the pinto and kidney beans, and cook, covered, for 30 minutes, stirring regularly.
Taste and adjust seasonings as needed before continuing to cook, uncovered, for another 15 minutes. Serve right away.

Calories:350| Fat: 27.8g | Carbs: 5.2g | Fiber: 2.9g| Sugars: 0.8 g | Protein: 24.9g

98. Red Bean Stew from Greece

Total Prep Time: 10 Minutes| Total Cook Time: 40 Minutes | Makes: 4 Servings

INGREDIENTS
1 tablespoon olive oil
1 yellow onion, chopped
2 carrots, cut into slices
2 garlic cloves, minced
1 sweet potato, peeled and diced
3 cups cooked dark red kidney beans, drained and rinsed
14.5-ounce can of diced tomatoes, drained
1 teaspoon hot or mild curry powder
1 teaspoon dried thyme
¼ teaspoon ground allspice
½ teaspoon salt
¼ teaspoon freshly ground black pepper
½ cup water
13.5-ounce can of coconut milk

DIRECTIONS
Heat the oil in a big saucepan over medium heat. Cover and cook the onion and carrots until they are cooked.
Mix in the garlic, sweet potato, and crushed red pepper.
Add the kidney beans, tomatoes, curry powder, thyme, allspice, salt, and black pepper and stir to combine.
Stir in the water, cover, and cook for 30 minutes, or until the veggies are soft.
Stir in the coconut milk and cook, uncovered, for 10 minutes.

Calories 160| Fat 3g (Saturated 0g) | Cholesterol 0mg| Sodium 549mg| Carbohydrate 30g| Dietary Fiber 5g| Protein 8g.

99. Edamame Donburi

Total Prep Time: 10 Minutes| Total Cook Time: 30 Minutes | Makes: 4 Servings

INGREDIENTS
1 cup fresh or frozen shelled edamame
1 tablespoon canola or grapeseed oil
1 yellow onion, minced
4 shiitake mushroom caps, sliced
1 teaspoon grated fresh ginger
2 green onions, minced
10 ounces firm tofu, drained and crumbled
2 tablespoons soy sauce
3 cups hot cooked white or brown rice
1 tablespoon toasted sesame oil
1 tablespoon toasted sesame seeds

DIRECTIONS
Cook the edamame in a saucepan of boiling salted water until soft, about 10 minutes.
Drain the water and set it aside.
Heat the canola oil in a skillet over medium heat.
Sauté the onion until it is cooked, about 5 minutes.
Cook for another 5 minutes, uncovered, with the mushrooms.
Add the ginger and green onions.
Add tofu and soy sauce and combine thoroughly for about 5 minutes.
Add the edamame and cook, stirring frequently.
Distribute the hot rice among four bowls, then top with the edamame and tofu combination and sesame oil.
Serve immediately with sesame seeds sprinkled on top.

Calories: 167|Fat: 5g|Saturated: 1g|Carbohydrate: 23g|Fiber: 3g|Protein: 6g

100. Stir-Fried Vegetables & Rice

Total Prep Time: 10 Minutes| Total Cook Time: 15 Minutes | Makes: 4 Servings

INGREDIENTS
2 tablespoons grapeseed oil
1 onion, finely chopped
1 carrot, finely chopped
1 zucchini, finely chopped
2 garlic cloves, minced
2 teaspoons grated fresh ginger
2 green onions, minced
½ teaspoon turmeric
3½ cups cold cooked long-grain rice
1 cup frozen peas, thawed
2 tablespoons soy sauce
2 teaspoons dry white wine
1 tablespoon toasted sesame oil

DIRECTIONS
Heat the oil in a skillet.
Stir-fry the onion, carrot, and zucchini for about 5 minutes, or until softened.
Stir in the garlic, ginger, and green onions for 3 minutes, or until softened.
If using, stir in the turmeric.
Stir in the rice, peas, soy sauce, and wine, for about 5 minutes.
Drizzle with sesame oil.

Calories 160| Fat 3g (Saturated 0g) | Cholesterol 0mg| Sodium 549mg| Carbohydrate 30g| Dietary Fiber 5g| Protein 8g.

101. Split Peas with Spinach

Total Prep Time: 10 Minutes| Total Cook Time: 2 Hours | Makes: 4 Servings

INGREDIENTS
1¼ cups yellow split peas, rinsed and drained
3½ cups water
1 teaspoon salt
cups fresh baby spinach
2 ripe plum tomatoes, finely chopped
¼ cup chopped fresh cilantro
1 tablespoon canola or grapeseed oil
2 garlic cloves, minced
1 tablespoon finely chopped fresh ginger
1 serrano or another hot green chile, seeded and minced
1 teaspoon ground cumin
½ teaspoon ground coriander
½ teaspoon turmeric
2 teaspoons fresh lemon juice

DIRECTIONS
Soak the split peas for 45 minutes in a medium dish of boiling water. Drain the water and place it in a big pot. Bring the water to a boil, then remove it from the heat. Cook, stirring occasionally until the split peas are soft and the sauce has thickened about 40 minutes.

Stir in the spinach, tomatoes, and cilantro until the spinach is wilted.

Heat the oil in a skillet over medium heat.

Add the garlic, ginger, and chile to a bowl. Heat for 1 minute, or until aromatic.

Remove the pan from the heat and toss in the cumin, coriander, turmeric, and lemon juice until thoroughly combined.

Stir the mixture into the dal to blend.

Serve right away.

Calories: 215, Total Fat: 7 g (Saturated Fat: 1.0 g), Sodium: 128 Mg, Total Carbohydrate: 36 g (Dietary Fiber: 9 g, Sugar: 14 g), Protein: 7 g

102. Lemon Pasta with Broccoli

Total Prep Time: 10 Minutes| Makes: 2 Servings

INGREDIENTS:
1 broccoli head
Handful of peas
2 garlic cloves
2 Servings of Spelt pasta, cooked
1 courgette
1 teaspoon of coconut oil
1 tomato
Pinch Himalayan salt & black pepper to taste
1/2 red onion
Juice of 1 lemon
2 bunches of rocket
Drizzle of olive oil

DIRECTIONS:
Sauté the broccoli, peas, garlic, red onion, and courgette in coconut oil.

Toss in the pasta along with the chopped tomato and rocket, and the lemon juice.

Calories 160| Fat 3g (Saturated 0g) | Cholesterol 0mg| Sodium 549mg| Carbohydrate 30g| Dietary Fiber 5g| Protein 8g.

103. Aubergine, Potato & Chickpea

Total Prep Time: 10 Minutes| Total Cook Time: 10 Minutes | Makes: 2 Servings

INGREDIENTS:
1 onion, peeled and finely sliced
1 teaspoon coriander
1 aubergine
1 potato
2 tablespoons coconut oil
1/2 teaspoons cumin
1 can chickpeas
1/4 teaspoons turmeric
Fresh coriander
SAUCE:
1 onion, peeled and finely sliced
2 teaspoons ginger, peeled and grated
6 whole cloves
450g plum tomatoes
1/4 teaspoons turmeric
2 tablespoons coconut oil
3 cloves garlic, crushed
1/2 teaspoons ground coriander
1/2 teaspoons ground cumin
1 1/2 teaspoons salt
1 teaspoon red chili powder, to taste

DIRECTIONS:
Sauté onion and cumin seeds for 3 minutes.
Add the potato, aubergine, chickpeas, ground coriander, cumin, and turmeric.
Cook the onion, garlic, ginger, and cloves for sixty seconds and then add the chopped tomatoes, turmeric, and other spices.
Blend the sauces with a hand blender until they are roughly blended. After that, add the vegetables, coriander, water, salt, and pepper to taste.
Finish with a sprinkling of fresh coriander and serve.

197 calories| Protein 7.8g| carbohydrates 24.2g | dietary fiber 3.7g | sugar 3.1 g | fat 8.3g | saturated fat 4.3g

104. Kale Slaw & Creamy Dressing

Total Prep Time: 15 Minutes| Makes: 2 Servings

INGREDIENTS:
1/3 cup sesame seeds
1 bell pepper
1/3 cup sunflower seeds
1 red onion
1 bunch of kale
4 cups of red cabbage, shredded
1 piece of root ginger
Fresh coriander
1 Serving cashew dressing

DIRECTIONS:
Toss all the ingredients together.

Calories 160| Fat 3g (Saturated 0g) | Cholesterol 0mg| Sodium 549mg| Carbohydrate 30g| Dietary Fiber 5g| Protein 8g.

105. Aubergine Mediterranean Chilli

Total Prep Time: 10 Minutes| Total Cook Time: 10 Minutes | Makes: 4 Servings

INGREDIENTS:
1 red onion, finely chopped
Coconut or olive oil
200g aubergine cut into cubes
2 garlic cloves, crushed
5 small red chilies, chopped OR
A dozen dried chilies
400g can of tomatoes
1/2 teaspoons ground
coriander
Pinch of ground cumin
Pinch of ground cinnamon
250g cooked black beans
Sea salt
Freshly ground black pepper
2 serves of brown rice, quinoa,
or couscous

DIRECTIONS:
In a separate pan, melt the coconut oil.
Fry the aubergines for another four minutes to soften and color them.
In the same pan, sauté the onions and garlic, then add the chiles and cook for a few minutes. After that, add the tomatoes, coriander, and spices, as well as the dried aubergine, and cook for around five or six minutes.
Add the black beans and continue to cook for another ten minutes while you prepare the brown rice/quinoa or couscous.

Calories 160| Fat 3g (Saturated 0g) | Cholesterol 0mg| Sodium 549mg| Carbohydrate 30g| Dietary Fiber 5g| Protein 8g

106. Brussels, Carrot & Greens

Total Prep Time: 10 Minutes| Total Cook Time: 10 Minutes | Makes: 4 Servings

INGREDIENTS:
1 broccoli
2 carrots, sliced thin
6 Brussels sprouts
2 cloves of garlic
1 teaspoon of caraway seeds
1/2 lemon
Peel 1 lemon Olive oil

DIRECTIONS:
Steam all the vegetables for 7 minutes on low heat.
Sauté garlic with caraway seeds, lemon peel, 1/2 lemon juice, and olive oil.
Add the carrot and Brussels sprouts.

Calories 160| Fat 3g (Saturated 0g) | Cholesterol 0mg| Sodium 549mg| Carbohydrate 30g| Dietary Fiber 5g| Protein 8g.

107. Broccoli Cauliflower Fry

Total Prep Time: 10 Minutes| Total Cook Time: 20 Minutes | Makes: 2 Servings

INGREDIENTS:
4 broccoli florets
4 cauliflower florets
1 pepper
Handful assorted sprouts
3 spring onions
1 garlic clove, chopped Liquid Aminos
Wild/brown rice

DIRECTIONS:
Cook the rice in a vegetable stock that is yeast-free.
Fry the garlic and onion in a steamer for three minutes.
Toss in the remaining ingredients and simmer for a few minutes more.

197 calories| Protein 7.8g| carbohydrates 24.2g | dietary fiber 3.7g | sugar 3.1 g | fat 8.3g | saturated fat 4.3g

108. Asparagus and Zucchini Pasta

Total Prep Time: 10 Minutes| Total Cook Time: 10 Minutes | Makes: 4 Servings

INGREDIENTS:
4 tomatoes, diced
1 zucchini
1/2 red onion, diced
1 bunch asparagus, steamed
200g of rocket
12 basil leaves
2 cloves garlic
4 servings of spelt pasta, cooked
Olive oil
DIRECTIONS:

Combine onion and tomatoes with handfuls of rocket, and asparagus and set them aside.
Blend remaining ingredients until a smooth, light green sauce forms.
Toss the pasta with the sauce, divide it into bowls, and top with the tomato, red onion, asparagus, and rocket.

Calories 160| Fat 3g (Saturated 0g) | Cholesterol 0mg| Sodium 549mg| Carbohydrate 30g| Dietary Fiber 5g| Protein 8g.

109. Veggie-Stuffed Tomatoes

Total Prep Time: 10 Minutes| Total Cook Time: 10 Minutes | Makes: 4 Servings

INGREDIENTS:
1 tablespoon cold-pressed oil
2 tomatoes
Half a small aubergine
1 onion
1/3 of a courgette
1-2 cloves of garlic
Pinch of sea salt and pepper
1 bunch of fresh spinach leaves

DIRECTIONS:
Preheat the oven to 160 degrees Celsius (325 degrees Fahrenheit).
Combine the vegetables with spinach, salt, and pepper, then drizzle with the oil.
After that, place the tomatoes on top and scoop out the center. Combine the middle piece with the rest of the mixture and stir well.
Now you must carefully place everything back into the tomatoes.
Put the tomatoes in a large pan with about 80ml of water and cover it with a lid once you're sure there's nothing else that could fit into them.
Bake for 18 minutes.

Calories 160| Fat 3g (Saturated 0g) | Cholesterol 0mg| Sodium 549mg| Carbohydrate 30g| Dietary Fiber 5g| Protein 8g.

110. Mediterranean Ratatouille

Total Prep Time: 10 Minutes| Total Cook Time: 3 Minutes | Makes: 4 Servings

INGREDIENTS:
2 bunches of baby spinach
3 aubergines, sliced
6 Pitted black olives
3 courgettes, sliced
2 red peppers
5 tomatoes, diced
3 teaspoons thyme leaves
2 cloves of garlic
Basil leaves
Coriander seeds
Drizzle extra virgin olive oil
Pinch Himalayan salt & black pepper

DIRECTIONS:
Remove the skins and dice the courgettes and aubergines to match.
In a skillet, heat a little olive or coconut oil and sauté one garlic bulb slowly.
Place the aubergine in a strainer and press with kitchen paper towels to remove any excess oil after cooking it all at once.
Heat more oil, then add the courgette and the other garlic.
Combine the remaining ingredients in a big pan and heat for 3 minutes.

197 calories| Protein 7.8g| carbohydrates 24.2g | dietary fiber 3.7g | sugar 3.1 g | fat 8.3g | saturated fat 4.3g

111. Mango, Jalapeno & Bean Salad

Total Prep Time: 10 Minutes| Makes: 6 Servings

INGREDIENTS:
15-ounce can, no-salt-added black beans, drained
1 bell pepper, seeded, cut into ½-inch pieces
1 cup avocado, cubed
2 green onions, sliced
15-ounce can, of low-sodium whole kernel corn
1 jalapeño pepper, diced
2 mangos, cut into ½-inch cubes
2 tablespoons fresh cilantro, chopped
1 tablespoon olive oil
1 teaspoon chili powder
1 teaspoon black pepper
2 tablespoons lime juice
1 teaspoon salt
Shredded lettuce

DIRECTIONS
Divide lettuce among 6 plated. Mix the black beans, corn, mango, avocado, onions, and jalapeno pepper. Blend the lime juice, olive oil, cilantro, chili powder, black pepper, and salt in a jar with a secure lid and shake vigorously to combine. Pour the mango-avocado mixture on top.
Drizzle over lettuce and mixed greens, gently tossing to coat.

Calories: 215, Total Fat: 7 g (Saturated Fat: 1.0 g), Sodium: 128 Mg, Total Carbohydrate: 36 g (Dietary Fiber: 9 g, Sugar: 14 g), Protein: 7 g

112. Spinach, Shrimp & Tangerine Bowl

Total Prep Time: 15 Minutes| Total Cook Time: 10 Minutes | Makes: 4 Servings

INGREDIENTS
1 cup endive
1 tablespoon parsley, chopped
1/4 small red onions, sliced in rings
3 cups spinach
1 tablespoon clarified butter
1/2 cup cooked shrimp (tails removed)
2 small tangerines, peeled and sectioned
1/4 cup roasted pine nuts
1 tablespoon basil, chopped
1 teaspoon fresh lime juice

DIRECTIONS
Combine the onion, spinach, endive, basil, and parsley in a large salad bowl.
Heat butter and cook the shrimp and lime together for one minute.
Toss the shrimp, pine nuts, and dressing of your choice into the salad bowl mix to combine.
Serve the salad with tangerine wedges as a garnish.

Calories 239| Fat 22g (Saturated 5g) | Cholesterol 35mg| Sodium 48mg| Carbohydrate 7g| Dietary Fiber 2g| Protein 7g.

113. Coral Lentil & Swiss Chard Soup

Total Prep Time: 5 Minutes| Total Cook Time: 30 Minutes | Makes: 4 Servings

INGREDIENTS:
1/2 teaspoon turmeric powder
2 tablespoons olive oil
2 carrots, diced
1/2 teaspoon ginger powder
3 garlic cloves, crushed
1 onion, diced
1 teaspoon cumin powder
1/2 teaspoon red pepper flakes
A 15-ounce can of diced
tomatoes
1 cup dried red lentils
2 liters of vegetable broth
1 bunch Swiss chard,
coarsely chopped

DIRECTIONS:
In a large soup or casserole dish, heat the oil.
Sauté onion and carrot for 7 minutes over medium-high heat.
Mix in garlic, cumin, ginger, turmeric, chili, and salt.
Cook for 5 minutes, scraping up any brown pieces from the bottom of the pan as you stir in the tomatoes until the liquid has reduced and the tomatoes are soft. Toss in the lentils and broth and cook, uncovered, for 10 minutes. Cook for another 5 minutes, stirring occasionally until the chard has wilted. Add salt and pepper to taste. Transfer to serving bowls, garnished with a wedge of lemon.

Calories 370|Total fat 9g|Saturated fat 5g|Total carbohydrate 57g|Dietary fiber 25g|Protein 20g

114. Fall Pumpkin Soup

Total Prep Time: 25 Minutes| Total Cook Time: 40 Minutes | Makes: 6 Servings

INGREDIENTS:
600 g pumpkin, peeled and
chopped
2 cups of vegetable broth
½ cup coconut milk
frying oil
1 tablespoon lemongrass,
chopped
1 ginger, peeled and grated
2 kaffir lime leaves, chopped
1 teaspoon of cumin
1 teaspoon coriander seeds
1 red pepper, seeded and
sliced
1 fresh turmeric, peeled and
sliced
Black pepper to taste

1 shallot, chopped
4 garlic cloves

DIRECTIONS:
Toss the squash in the oil before placing it on the baking sheet and roasting until golden brown. In a pan, heat the oil and sauté the shallots until brown. Add cumin and coriander. Add the kaffir leaves, turmeric, ginger, lemongrass, and chili, and cook for another minute, stirring to avoid burning Add the squash to the broth then cover and cook Reduce the heat to low and cook for an additional 10 minutes. Add the coconut milk and increase the heat again to simmer for 7 minutes.

Calories: 192 | Fat: 15g

115. Barley Vegetable Soup

Total Prep Time: 5 Minutes| Total Cook Time: 40 Minutes | Makes: 6 Servings

INGREDIENTS:
1 cup celery, chopped
1 cup carrots, chopped
1 sprig of rosemary
1 clove of garlic, minced
3/4 cup peeled barley
4 cups vegetable broth
1 can of tomato puree (28 oz.)
1 can of beans, drained and rinsed (15 oz.)
2 cups kale, coarsely chopped
Grated vegan parmesan

DIRECTIONS:
In a saucepan, sauté the onions, carrots, and celery with olive oil (extra-virgin).
Cook for another 3 minutes after adding the rosemary, garlic, and barley.
Bring the broth to a boil, constantly stirring.
Reduce the heat to low, and cook for about 1 hour until the barley is cooked, then add the tomatoes and beans.
Serve with vegan parmesan.

Calories: 277.37|Carbs: 52.82g|Protein: 7.43g|Fats: 5.9g| Fiber: 9.1g

116. Squash and Lentil Soup

Total Prep Time: 10 Minutes| Total Cook Time: 40 Minutes | Makes: 4-6 Servings

INGREDIENTS:
8 cups of vegetable broth
1 large onion, diced
1 peeled and diced butternut squash
1 cup brown lentils
2 teaspoons minced garlic
1 bay leaf
1/2 teaspoon ground nutmeg
1 cup spinach, chopped
1/2 teaspoon of salt

DIRECTIONS:
Add all ingredients except spinach to your slow cooker and mix well.
Cook 3 to 4 hours on high power or 8 hours on low.
Remove the bay leaf.
Add chopped spinach and stir until softened.

Calories: 167|Fat: 5g|Saturated: 1g|Carbohydrate: 23g|Fiber: 3g|Protein: 6g

117. Rosemary Pasta Shells Soup

Total Prep Time: 8 Minutes| Total Cook Time: 25 Minutes | Makes: 4 Servings

INGREDIENTS
2 teaspoons olive oil
1⁄2 cup whole wheat pasta shells
4 cups fat-free chicken broth
1 garlic clove, finely minced
1 dash crushed red pepper flakes
1 shallot, finely diced
1 teaspoon rosemary
3 Cups Baby Spinach, cleaned and trimmed
1⁄8 teaspoon black pepper
14.5-ounce can of diced tomatoes
14.5-ounce can of white beans

DIRECTIONS
Preheat the oven to 350°F.
In a pot, heat the oil.
Add the garlic and shallot and cook for 4 minutes.
Add the broth, tomatoes, beans, rosemary, and black and red pepper to taste.
Cook until they begin to boil.
Add the noodles.
Stir in the spinach and cook until it has wilted.
Calories 218.4, Fat 3.3 g, Carbohydrates 37.9 g, Protein 12 g

118. Bell Pasta with Kidney Beans

Total Prep Time: 10 Minutes| Total Cook Time: 40 Minutes | Makes: 8 Servings

INGREDIENTS
1 tablespoon olive oil
1 1/2 cup kidney beans, cooked
1 onion, chopped
2 teaspoon chopped fresh thyme
2 cloves garlic, minced
1/2 cup chopped spinach
1 red bell pepper, chopped
1 cup seashell pasta
3 C. low fat, low chicken broth
Pinch ground black pepper to taste
1 cup canned whole tomatoes, chopped

DIRECTIONS
Preheat a pot.
Heat oil and cook onion, bell pepper, and garlic for 3 minutes.
Mix in the broth, tomatoes, and beans.
Reduce the heat to low and cook the soup for 20 minutes.
Mix in the thyme, spinach, and pasta and cook another 5 minutes.
Season the soup with salt and pepper as needed.
Calories 174 kcal, Fat 3.1 g, Carbohydrates 29g, Protein 8 g

119. Rigatoni Pasta Casserole

Total Prep Time: 30 Minutes| Total Cook Time: 55 Minutes | Makes: 6 Servings

INGREDIENTS
1 lb. ground sausage
1⁄4 cup Romano cheese, grated
28-ounce can of Italian-style tomato sauce
chopped parsley, to garnish
14-ounce can cannellini beans, drained
and rinsed
16-ounce rigatoni pasta, cooked
1⁄2 teaspoon minced garlic
1 teaspoon Italian seasoning
3 cups shredded mozzarella cheese

DIRECTIONS
Preheat the oven to 350 degrees Fahrenheit.
Using butter or oil, grease a casserole dish.
In a pre-heated pot, cook garlic and sausages for 6 minutes.
Add tomato sauce, beans, and Italian spice, and cook for 5 minutes on low heat.
Half of the sausage pasta mixture should be poured into the oiled casserole, followed by half of the mozzarella cheese.
To make another layer, repeat the process.
Place a piece of foil on top of the dish and top it with Romano cheese.
Bake the rigatoni casserole for 26 minutes.

Calories 795.6, Fat 37.6 g, Cholesterol 166.2 mg, Sodium 1842.2 mg, Carbohydrates 73.2, Protein 41.2 g

120. Farfalle Pasta with Mushrooms

Total Prep Time: 10 Minutes| Total Cook Time: 35 Minutes | Makes: 4 Servings

INGREDIENTS
1 lb. farfalle pasta, cooked
8-ounce package of mushrooms, sliced
1/3 cup olive oil
1 tablespoon dried oregano
1 clove of garlic, chopped
1 tablespoon paprika
1/4 cup butter
Pinch salt and pepper to taste
2 zucchinis, quartered and sliced
1 onion, chopped
1 tomato, chopped

DIRECTIONS
Fry garlic, mushrooms, onion, and tomato in olive oil for 17 minutes.
Season with salt, pepper, paprika, and oregano.
Combine the vegetables and noodles in a mixing bowl.

Calories 717 kcal, Carbohydrates 92.8 g, Cholesterol 31 mg, Fat 32.9 g, Protein 18.1 g, Sodium 491 mg

121. Tortellini Salad with Spinach

Total Prep Time: 20 Minutes| Total Cook Time: 40 Minutes | Makes: 2 Servings

INGREDIENTS
9-ounce package of spinach and cheese
1 jar tortellini, cooked
Pinch salt and ground black pepper to taste
4-ounce jar pesto
1/4 cup halved, seeded, and sliced cucumber
1/4 cup halved cherry tomatoes
1/4 cup red onion, diced
1/2 Cup chopped mache

DIRECTIONS
Place the cucumbers, tomatoes, onions, tortellini, and mache on top of the pesto in the jar. Add a little salt and pepper to taste.
Serve your salad right immediately or keep it refrigerated until ready to eat.

Calories 719 kcal, Fat 39.1 g, Carbohydrates 66.6g, Protein 29.2 g, Cholesterol 76 mg, Sodium 1027 mg

122. Egg Noodles with Croutons

Total Prep Time: 5 Minutes| Total Cook Time: 20 Minutes | Makes: 4 Servings

INGREDIENTS
12 oz. egg noodles, cooked
1 pinch salt
1/2 cup unsalted butter
1/4 teaspoon pepper
2 slices of white bread, torn

DIRECTIONS
Melt the butter in a frying pan over medium heat and cook the bread pieces until crispy.
Remove the pan from the heat and add salt and black pepper.
Combine the noodles and croutons in a serving bowl.

Calories 565.3, Fat 27.2g, Cholesterol 132.8mg, Sodium 145.0mg, Carbohydrates 67.3g, Protein 13.3g

123. Snow Peas & Spaghetti

Total Prep Time: 20 Minutes| Total Cook Time: 40 Minutes | Makes: 6 Servings

INGREDIENTS
8 oz. spaghetti, cooked
1 tablespoon canola oil
1 tablespoons cornstarch
2 cups fresh snow peas
4 tablespoons reduced-sodium soy sauce,
2 cups carrots, shredded
3 green onions, chopped
2 tablespoons sesame oil, divided
3/8 teaspoon ground ginger, minced
1 lb. boneless skinless chicken breast,
1/2 teaspoon crushed red pepper flakes
2 tablespoons white vinegar
1 tablespoon sugar

DIRECTIONS
Combine the cornstarch, half the soy sauce, and sesame oil in a mixing bowl.
Place the chicken in a zip-top bag and pour the sesame oil sauce over it.
Shake the bag to coat it and press it to seal it.
Set it aside for 20 minutes to absorb the flavors.
To prepare the sauce, combine the vinegar, sugar, remaining soy sauce, and sesame oil.
Preheat a skillet over .and heat the canola oil.
Cook chicken for 8 minutes and then add in the carrots and peas.
Add the green onions, ginger, and pepper flakes and mix well. A
Combine the cooked chicken, vinegar sauce, and pasta in a mixing bowl.
Cook for 2 minutes before serving.

Calories 337.1, Fat 9.5g, Cholesterol 48.4mg, Sodium 477.5mg, Carbohydrates 38.9g, Protein 22.7g

124. Garlic and Sesame Noodles

Total Prep Time: 5 Minutes| Total Cook Time: 10 Minutes | Makes: 4 Servings

INGREDIENTS:
1-pound brown rice spaghetti, cooked
1½ tablespoons toasted sesame oil
1 cup sliced green onions
7 garlic cloves, crushed
¼ cup soy sauce
¼ cup hazelnut sugar
2 tablespoons rice vinegar
½ teaspoon red pepper flakes
Sesame seeds for garnish

DIRECTIONS:
Over low to medium heat, heat a skillet.
Pour in the sesame oil and once heated, stir in ¾ cup of green onions, garlic, and red pepper flakes.
Cook until garlic is lightly browned and fragrant, stirring frequently to avoid burning.
Add soy sauce, coconut sugar, and rice vinegar and stir to combine. Add the prepared, drained pasta and toss to coat with the sauce.
Let the noodles cook for 1-2 minutes or until heated through.
Garnish with the remaining ¼ cup of sliced green onions and a few sesame seeds.

Calories: 305KCAL | Carbohydrates: 47g | Protein: 7.2g | Fat: 12.8g | Fiber: 2.5g

125. Vegetable Mediterranean Pasta

Total Prep Time: 10 Minutes| Total Cook Time: 10 Minutes | Makes: 4 Servings

INGREDIENTS:
1/2 pack of vegetable or spelt pasta, cooked
1 courgette
1 medium broccoli
5 garlic gloves
Chilies, diced
4 tomatoes
A handful of basil leaves
1 tablespoon of olive oil
Himalayan salt and black pepper.

DIRECTIONS:
Heat the oil on a low, gentle heat, and sauté the garlic, basil, and chili for two minutes.
Add the remaining vegetables, which have been sliced to make them tiny and easy to cook.
Combine everything, including the pasta, and stir for another two minutes.
Salt and pepper to taste, then serve.

Calories 160| Fat 3g (Saturated 0g) | Cholesterol 0mg| Sodium 549mg| Carbohydrate 30g| Dietary Fiber 5g| Protein 8g.

126. Tomato & Cauliflower Spaghetti

Total Prep Time: 5 Minutes| Total Cook Time: 5 Minutes | Makes: 4 Servings

INGREDIENTS:
A handful of cauliflower, chopped small
1 tablespoon olive oil
1 garlic clove, finely chopped
125g sun-blushed tomatoes, chopped
1 shallot, finely chopped
Large handful of rocket
Handful chive, chopped well
½ lemon, juice only
Large handful of spinach
250g spelt or wheat-free spaghetti, cooked

DIRECTIONS:
Heat the coconut oil and sauté the shallot, garlic, and tomatoes very gently.
Add the lemon juice.
Serve on top of the spaghetti.

157 calories| Protein 7.8g| carbohydrates 24.2g | dietary fiber 3.7g | sugar 3.1 g | fat 8.3g | saturated fat

127. Cheddar and Bell Pepper Pizza

Total Prep Time: 10 Minutes| Total Cook Time: 20 Minutes | Makes: 2 Servings

INGREDIENTS
Pizza dough
4 oz. Shredded Cheddar Cheese
1 Vine Tomato
1/4 cup Tomato Sauce
2/3 Bell Pepper
2-3 tablespoons Fresh Basil

DIRECTIONS
Preheat the oven to 350°F and bake the dough for 10 minutes.
Slice vine tomato and place on each pizza dough, along with 2 tablespoons tomato sauce.
Top with shredded Cheddar cheese and bell peppers.
Return to the oven for another 10 minutes.
Take the pizzas out of the oven and set them aside to cool.
Serve it up with a sprig of fresh basil on top.

410 Calories, 33g Fats, 3g Carbohydrates, and 28g Protein.

128. Mediterranean Flatbread Pizza

Total Prep Time: 10 Minutes| Total Cook Time: 22 Minutes | Makes: 2 Servings

INGREDIENTS
PEANUT SAUCE

4 tablespoons PBFit
2 tablespoons Rice Wine Vinegar
4 tablespoons Soy Sauce
4 tablespoons Reduced Sugar Ketchup
4 tablespoons Coconut Oil
1 teaspoon Fish Sauce
Juice of 1/2 Lime
Pizza Base
TOPPINGS
2 Chicken Thighs, cooked
3 oz. Mung Bean Sprouts
6 oz. Mozzarella Cheese
2 Green Onions
1 1/2 oz. Shredded Carrot
2 tablespoons Peanuts, chopped
3 tablespoons Cilantro, chopped

DIRECTIONS
Preheat the oven to 400 degrees Fahrenheit. Whisk together all of the sauce components. Mix the egg into the cheese thoroughly. Then, completely combine the dry ingredients with the cheese. Place the pizza base on a Silpat and press it from edge to edge to make a huge rectangle. Place the pizza in the oven for 14 minutes, or until the top is nicely browned. Set aside the pre-cooked chicken, which has been chopped into bite-size parts.

Turn the pizza over, so the bottom is now facing up. Sauce, chicken, shredded carrots, and mozzarella go on top of the pizza. Return to the oven for another 8 minutes, or until the cheese has melted. Garnish with mung bean sprouts, sliced spring onion, chopped peanuts, and cilantro.

268 Calories, 21g Fats, 2g Carbohydrates, and 15g Protein.

129. Ham and Cheese Stromboli

Total Prep Time: 10 Minutes| Total Cook Time: 20 Minutes | Makes: 4 Servings

INGREDIENTS
1 teaspoon Italian Seasoning
2 cups Mozzarella Cheese, shredded
4 tablespoons Almond Flour
3 tablespoons Coconut Flour
1 Egg
4 oz. Ham
5 oz. Cheddar Cheese
Salt and Pepper to Taste

DIRECTIONS
In a mixing dish, combine almond and coconut flour, as well as your seasonings. Start incorporating the melted mozzarella into your flour mixture. Add your egg and stir everything together. Transfer the dough to a flat surface with parchment paper. Place the second sheet of parchment paper on top of the dough ball and flatten it out with a rolling pin. Cut diagonal lines from the edges of the dough to the center with a pizza cutter. Alternate between ham and cheddar on the uncut dough stretch. Then, one slice of dough at a time, lift it and place it on top of the filling, covering it completely. Bake for around 20 minutes, or until it has gone golden brown.

300 Calories, 28g Fats, 7g Carbohydrates, 26g Protein

130. Mini Portobello Pizzas

Total Prep Time: 10 Minutes| Total Cook Time: 12 Minutes | Makes: 4 Servings

INGREDIENTS
1/4 Cup Fresh Chopped Basil
4 Portobello Mushroom Caps
1 Vine Tomato, sliced thin
Pinch Salt and Pepper to Taste
4 oz. Fresh Mozzarella Cheese
6 tablespoons Olive Oil
20 slices Pepperoni

DIRECTIONS
Scrape out all of the mushroom's insides.
Preheat the oven to high broil and brush the insides of the mushrooms with Olive Oil. Season with salt and pepper.
Broil the mushroom for 3 minutes.
Turn the mushrooms over and brush with Olive Oil once more.
Season with salt and pepper and broil the mushrooms for a further 4 minutes.
In each mushroom, place a tomato and basil leaf.
Top each mushroom with 5 pieces of pepperoni and fresh cubed mozzarella cheese.
Broil for another 2 minutes, or until the cheese is melted and browning.

320 Calories, 31g Fats, 8g Carbohydrates, 5g Protein.

131. Rotisserie Chicken Pizza

Total Prep Time: 10 Minutes| Total Cook Time: 13 Minutes | Makes: 4 Servings

INGREDIENTS
Dairy-Free Pizza Crust
6 Eggs
6 tablespoons Parmesan Cheese, shredded
3 tablespoons Psyllium Husk Powder
1 1/2 teaspoon Italian Seasoning
Salt and Pepper to Taste
TOPPINGS
4 oz. Cheddar Cheese, shredded
6 oz. Rotisserie Chicken, shredded
1 tablespoons Mayonnaise
4 tablespoons BBQ Sauce
4 tablespoons Tomato Sauce

DIRECTIONS
Preheat the oven to 425 degrees Fahrenheit.
Combine all of the crust ingredients in an immersion blender.
Using a silicone spatula, spread the dough out on a Silpat.
Place the crust in the oven and bake for 10 minutes.
Flip the pizza once it's finished in the oven.
Add your chosen toppings and bake for another 3 minutes under the broiler.

356 Calories, 25g Fats, 9g Carbohydrates, 25g Protein.

132. Olive Pizza bombs

Total Prep Time: 10 Minutes | Makes: 2 Servings

INGREDIENTS
4 oz. Cream Cheese
4 slices Pepperoni, diced
4 pitted Black Olives, diced
2 tablespoons Sun-Dried Tomato Pesto

DIRECTIONS
Combine basil, tomato pesto, and cream cheese in a mixing bowl.
Mix in the olives and pepperoni.
Form into balls and garnish with pepperoni, basil, and olives.

110 Calories, 5g Fats, 3g Carbohydrates, 3g Protein.

133. Tofu and Capers Pizza

Total Prep Time: 10 Minutes| Total Cook Time: 15 Minutes | Makes: 4 Servings

INGREDIENTS
2 tablespoons olive oil
16-ounce package of tofu, drained and sliced
Pinch Salt
3 garlic cloves, minced
14.5-ounce can of diced tomatoes, drained
¼ cup sun-dried tomatoes, sliced
1 tablespoon capers
1 teaspoon dried oregano
½ teaspoon sugar
Freshly ground black pepper
2 tablespoons minced fresh parsley

DIRECTIONS
Preheat the oven to 275 degrees Fahrenheit.
Heat oil in a skillet and cook tofu, until the tofu, is golden brown on both sides.
Season the tofu with salt and pepper to taste.
Heat the remaining oil in the same skillet.
Add garlic and cook for 1 minute until the garlic is softened.
Add the diced tomatoes, sun-dried tomatoes, olives, and capers and stir to combine.
Toss in the oregano, sugar, and salt, then season to taste with pepper.
Cook for around ten minutes.
Drizzle the sauce over the fried tofu slices and garnish with parsley. Serve right away.

Calories 795.6, Fat 37.6 g, Cholesterol 166.2 mg, Sodium 1842.2 mg, Carbohydrates 73.2, Protein 41.2 g

134. Cheesy Ramen Pizzas

Total Prep Time: 10 Minutes| Total Cook Time: 30 Minutes | Makes: 4 Servings

INGREDIENTS
6 oz. ramen noodles, any flavor
2 cups mozzarella cheese, grated
OTHER TOPPINGS
1/2 cup milk
4 black olives
1 egg, beaten
1 cup mushroom
1/4 cup Parmesan cheese, grated
canned jalapeño slices
1 cup barbecue sauce
1 cup bell pepper
1 cup cooked chicken, chopped
1 teaspoon red pepper flakes
1/2 red onion, sliced thinly
11-ounce mandarin oranges drained well

DIRECTIONS
Preheat your oven to 350 degrees F.
Cook the ramen noodles in a pan of salted boiling water for about 3 minutes.
Drain and set aside.
Whisk together the egg, milk, and Parmesan cheese in a mixing dish.
Stir in the noodles until everything is well combined.
Evenly distribute the noodle mixture on a prepared pan.
Cook for around 12 minutes in the oven.
Sprinkle the barbecue sauce over the noodles, then add the chicken, onions, and oranges.
Evenly sprinkle the mozzarella cheese on top.
Cook for around 15 minutes in the oven.

Calories 577.9, Fat 27.6g, Cholesterol 133.1mg, Sodium1510.0mg, Carbohydrates 50.6g, Protein 31.9g

135. Pizza Breadsticks

Total Prep Time: 14 Minutes| Total Cook Time: 20 Minutes | Makes: 4 Servings

INGREDIENTS
BREADSTICK BASE
2 cups Mozzarella Cheese, melted
3/4 cup Almond Flour
1 tablespoon Psyllium Husk Powder
3 tablespoons Cream Cheese
1 Egg
1 teaspoon Baking Powder
2 tablespoons Italian Seasoning
1 teaspoon salt
1 teaspoon Pepper
EXTRA TOPPINGS
1 teaspoon Garlic Powder
1 teaspoon Onion Powder
3 oz. Cheddar Cheese
1/4 cup Parmesan Cheese

DIRECTIONS
Preheat the oven to 400 degrees Fahrenheit.
Combine the egg and cream cheese in a mixing bowl.
Combine all of the dry ingredients in a mixing bowl: almond flour, Psyllium husk, and baking powder.
Mix the mozzarella cheese with the egg, cream cheese, and dry ingredients.
Knead the dough together with your hands. Set it on a Silpat.
Press the dough flat until it covers the entire baking sheet.
Transfer the dough to foil so you can cut it with a pizza cutter.
Cut the dough into pieces and season it with salt and pepper.
Bake until crisp, for 14 minutes.

Calories 719 kcal, Fat 39.1 g, Carbohydrates 66.6g, Protein 29.2 g, Cholesterol 76 mg, Sodium 1027 mg

136. Easy Peasy Pizza

Total Prep Time: 10 Minutes| Total Cook Time: 20 Minutes | Makes: 2 Servings

INGREDIENTS
PIZZA CRUST
2 Eggs
2 tablespoons Parmesan Cheese
1 tablespoon Psyllium Husk Powder
1/2 teaspoon Italian Seasoning
Salt to Taste
2 teaspoon Frying Oil
TOPPINGS
5 oz. Mozzarella Cheese
3 tablespoons Low-Carb Tomato Sauce
1 tablespoon Freshly Chopped Basil

DIRECTIONS
In a mixing dish, combine all of the dry ingredients.
Using your immersion blender, combine 2 eggs with the rest of the ingredients. Heat 2 teaspoons of frying oil.
Fill the pan halfway with the ingredients and spread it out into a circle. Flip the pizza crust once the edges have started to set and look slightly golden. In the oven, preheat the broiler to high. Cook for 50 seconds on the other side.
Brush low-carb tomato sauce over the pizza top with cheese and place the pizza in the oven to broil until it's bubbling.

459 Calories, 35g Fats, 5g Carbohydrates, 27g Protein.

137. Raspberry Lemon Popsicles

Total Prep Time: 2 Hours | Makes: 6 Servings

INGREDIENTS
100G Raspberries
Juice 1/2 Lemon
1/4 cup Coconut Oil
1 cup Coconut Milk
1/4 cup Sour Cream
1/4 cup Heavy Cream
1/2 teaspoon Guar Gum
20 drops of Liquid Stevia

DIRECTIONS
Combine all ingredients in a jar and combine with an immersion blender.Blend until the raspberries are thoroughly combined with the remaining ingredients. Strain the mixture, ensuring that all raspberry seeds are removed. I tried making a batch with the seeds still in it, and as I ate it, they began to bother my tongue. Fill the molds with the mixture. Freeze the popsicles for at least 2 hours before serving. To remove the popsicles from the mold, run them under hot water.

156 Calories, 16g Fats, 2g Carbohydrates, 0.5g Protein.

138. Napolitan Bombs

Total Prep Time: 2 Hours| Makes: 24 bombs

INGREDIENTS
1/2 cup butter
1/2 cup Coconut Oil
1/2 cup Sour Cream
1/2 cup Cream Cheese
2 tablespoons Erythritol
25 drops of Liquid Stevia
2 tablespoons Cocoa Powder
1 teaspoon Vanilla Extract
2 Strawberries

DIRECTIONS
Combine the butter, coconut oil, sour cream, cream cheese, erythritol, and liquid stevia in a mixing dish.
Blend the ingredients in an immersion blender until smooth. Separate the mixture into three bowls. Toss the cocoa powder in one bowl, the strawberries in another, and the vanilla in the third. Using an immersion blender, combine all of the ingredients once more. Pour the chocolate mixture into a spout-equipped container.
Fill a fat bomb mold halfway with the chocolate mixture. Freeze for 30 minutes before repeating with the vanilla mixture. Freeze the vanilla mixture for 30 minutes before continuing with the strawberry mixture. Freeze for at least 1 hour more. Remove them from the fat bomb molds once they've totally frozen.

102 Calories, 9g Fats, 0.4g Carbohydrates, and 0.6g Protein.

139. Coconut Orange Creamsicle Bombs

Total Prep Time: 2 Hours | Makes: 10 Servings

INGREDIENTS
1/2 cup Coconut Oil
1/2 cup Heavy Whipping Cream
4 oz. Cream Cheese
1 teaspoon Orange Vanilla Mio
drops Liquid Stevia

DIRECTIONS
Combine the coconut oil, heavy cream, and cream cheese in a mixing bowl.
To combine all of the ingredients, use an immersion blender.
Combine the Orange Vanilla Mio and liquid stevia in a mixing bowl and stir well.
Freeze the mixture for 2 hours on a silicone dish.
Remove off the silicone tray once it has firm and place in the freezer.

172 Calories, 20g Fats, 0.7g Carbohydrates, 1g Protein.

140. Cocoa Peanut Butter Bombs

Total Prep Time: 20 Minutes | Makes: 8 bombs

INGREDIENTS
1/2 cup Coconut Oil
1/4 cup Cocoa Powder
2 tablespoons PB Fit Powder
2 tablespoons Shelled Hemp Seeds
2 tablespoons Heavy Cream
1 teaspoon Vanilla Extract
28 drops of Liquid Stevia
1/4 cup Unsweetened Shredded Coconut

DIRECTIONS
Combine all of the dry ingredients and the coconut oil in a mixing bowl.
Combine the heavy cream, vanilla, and liquid stevia in a mixing bowl. Remix until everything is well incorporated and the texture is somewhat creamy.
On a plate, pour unsweetened shredded coconut
Roll out the balls with your hands, then roll them in unsweetened shredded coconut. Place on a parchment paper-lined baking tray.
Set aside for about 20 minutes in the freezer.

207 Calories, 20g Fats, 0.8g Carbohydrates, 4g Protein.

141. Tortilla Chips

Total Prep Time: 10 Minutes| Total Cook Time: 5 Minutes | Makes: 6 Servings

INGREDIENTS
TORTILLA CHIPS
Flaxseed Tortillas
Oil for Deep Frying
Salt and Pepper to Taste
TOPPINGS
Diced Jalapeno
Fresh Salsa
Shredded Cheese
Full-Fat Sour Cream

DIRECTIONS
Preheat the deep fryer to 350°F.
Place the tortilla pieces in the basket.
Fry for 2 minutes before flipping on the other side for another 2 minutes.
Remove from the fryer and set aside to cool on paper towels.
Season with salt and pepper.
Serve with your favorite toppings!

1g Fats, 0.04g Carbohydrates 0g, 0.9g Protein.

142. Jalapeno Popper Bombs

Total Prep Time: 10 Minutes| Makes: 2 Servings

INGREDIENTS
3 oz. Cream Cheese
3 slices Bacon, cooked crisp
1 Jalapeno Pepper, sliced
1/2 teaspoon Dried Parsley
1/4 teaspoon Onion Powder
1/4 teaspoon Garlic Powder
Salt and Pepper to Taste

DIRECTIONS
Combine cream cheese, jalapeno, and spices in a mixing bowl.
Season with salt and pepper.
Mix in the bacon grease until it forms a firm consistency.
Place crumbled bacon on a platter. Using your hands, form the cream cheese mixture into balls, then roll the balls in bacon.

200 Calories, 13g Fats, 5g Net Carb, 8g Protein.

143. Personal Pan Pizza Dip

Total Prep Time: 10 Minutes| Total Cook Time: 20 Minutes | Makes: 1 Serving

INGREDIENTS
6 oz. Cream Cheese microwaved
1/4 cup Sour Cream
1/4 cup Mayonnaise
1/2 cup Mozzarella Cheese, shredded
Salt and Pepper to Taste
1/2 cup Low-Carb Tomato Sauce
1/2 cup Mozzarella Cheese, shredded
1/4 cup Parmesan Cheese

DIRECTIONS
Preheat the oven to 350 degrees Fahrenheit.
In a mixing bowl, combine the cream cheese, sour cream, mayonnaise, and mozzarella cheese.
Season with salt and pepper.
Pour the mixture into four ramekins.
Spread Tomato Sauce generously over each ramekin as well as mozzarella cheese and parmesan cheese, then top your pan pizza dips with your favorite toppings.
Bake for 20 minutes, or until the cheese has melted and started to bubble.
Serve alongside some tasty breadsticks or pork rinds!

349 Calories, 35g Fats, 4g Carbohydrates, 14g Protein.

144. Corndog Muffins

Total Prep Time: 10 Minutes| Total Cook Time: 15 Minutes | Makes: 10 Servings

INGREDIENTS
1/2 cup Blanched Almond Flour
1/2 cup Flaxseed Meal
1 tablespoon Psyllium Husk Powder
3 tablespoons Swerve Sweetener
1/4 teaspoon salt
1/4 teaspoon Baking Powder
1/4 cup butter, melted
1 Egg
1/3 cup Sour Cream
1/4 cup Coconut Milk
10 Smokies (or 3 hot dogs)

DIRECTIONS
Preheat the oven to 375 degrees Fahrenheit.
In a mixing dish, combine all of the dry ingredients.
Mix in the egg, sour cream, and butter until thoroughly combined.
Mix in the coconut milk.
Cut the Smokies in half and place them in the center of the batter.
Bake for 12 minutes, then broil for 2 minutes, or until gently browned on top.
Allow the muffins to cool in the tray for a few minutes before removing them to cool on a wire rack.
Serve with spring onion as a garnish.

77 Calories, 8g Fats, 0.7g Carbohydrates, 4.1g Protein.

145. Layered Fried Queso Blanco

Total Prep Time: 10 Minutes| Total Cook Time: 20 Minutes | Makes: 1 Serving

INGREDIENTS
6 oz. Queso Blanco, cubed
1 1/2 tablespoons Olive Oil
2 oz. Olives
Pinch Red Pepper Flakes

DIRECTIONS
In a skillet over medium-high heat, heat the oil.
Add the cheese cubes and allow them to partially melt.
Continue to heat the cheese, then fold half of it in on itself.
Continue to flip the cheese and heat it until a beautiful crust forms.
Form a block with the melted cheese and seal all of the corners with another spatula, fork, or knife.
Remove the pan from the heat.
Cut the cheese into cubes with a knife.
Serve with a drizzle of olive oil and a sprinkling of red pepper flakes on top.

520 Calories, 43g Fats, 2g Carbohydrates, 30g Protein.

146. Berry & Almond Fruit Wrap

Total Prep Time: 10 Minutes| Makes: 2 Servings

INGREDIENTS:
1 tortilla, preferably whole wheat
2 teaspoons strawberry preserves
½ cup sliced fresh strawberries
2 tablespoons reduced-fat ricotta cheese
2 tablespoons sliced almonds, toasted

DIRECTIONS
Spread the preserves on the tortilla after toasting it.
Serve with a dollop of Ricotta cheese on top.
Arrange the cut fruit and almonds on top.
Roll tightly.

Calories: 300, Fat: 11 g (Saturated Fat: 3 g, Unsaturated Fat: 5 g), Cholesterol: 8 Mg Sodium: 455 Mg, Total Carbohydrate: 45 g (Dietary Fiber: 4 g, Sugar: 18 g), Protein: 12 g

147. No-Bake Pumpkin Cheesecake

Total Prep Time: 20 Minutes + Freezing Time | Makes: 2 Servings

INGREDIENTS
FOR THE CRUST
3/4 cup Almond Flour
1/2 cup Flaxseed Meal
1/4 cup butter
1 teaspoon Pumpkin Pie Spice
25 drops of Liquid Stevia
FOR THE FILLING
6 oz. Cream Cheese
1/3 cup Pumpkin Puree
2 tablespoons Sour Cream
1/4 cup Heavy Cream
3 tablespoons Butter
1/4 teaspoon Pumpkin Pie Spice
25 drops of Liquid Stevia

DIRECTIONS
Mix all of the crust's dry ingredients thoroughly.
Mash together the dry ingredients with the butter and liquid stevia until a dough forms.
Place the dough in your mini tart pans.
Press the dough up the side of the tart pan until it reaches the top.
To make the filling, combine all of the ingredients in a mixing bowl.
Blend the filling ingredients using an immersion blender.
Place the crust in the refrigerator for at least 4 hours.
Remove from the fridge, slice, and top with whipped cream.
266 Calories, 23g Fats, 3g Carbohydrates, 4g Protein.

148. Crusty Peanut Butter Bars

Total Prep Time: 10 Minutes| Total Cook Time: 15 Minutes | Makes: 2 Servings

INGREDIENTS
CRUST
1 cup Almond Flour
1/4 cup butter, melted
1/2 teaspoon Cinnamon
1 tablespoon Erythritol
Pinch of Salt
FUDGE
1/4 cup Heavy Cream
1/4 cup butter, melted
1/2 cup Peanut Butter
1/4 cup Erythritol
1/2 teaspoon Vanilla Extract
1/8 teaspoon Xanthan Gum
TOPPING
1/3 cup Chocolate, Chopped

DIRECTIONS
Preheat the oven to 400 degrees Fahrenheit.
Combine the almond flour with half of the melted butter in a mixing bowl. Stir in the erythritol and cinnamon. Press into the bottom of a baking dish lined with parchment paper.
Bake the crust for 10 minutes, or until golden brown around the edges.
In a food processor, blend all of the fudge ingredients for the filling. Spread the fudge layer carefully up the sides of the baking dish after the crust has cooled.
Top your bars with chopped chocolate just before cooling.
Remove the bars by peeling the parchment paper out once they have cooled.
Calories 795.6, Fat 37.6 g, Cholesterol 166.2 mg, Sodium 1842.2 mg, Carbohydrates 73.2, Protein 41.2 g

149. Pumpkin and Date Ice Cream

Total Prep Time: 15 Minutes + Freezing Time| Makes: 6 Servings

INGREDIENTS:
½ teaspoon vanilla extract
15 ounces pumpkin puree
2 cans of unsweetened coconut milk
½ cup dates, pitted and chopped
½ teaspoon ground cinnamon
1½ teaspoons pumpkin pie spice

DIRECTIONS:
Blend all the ingredients until smooth.
Freeze for up to 2 hours.
Pour the mixture into an ice cream machine halfway and process.
Freeze the ice cream for around 1 to 2 hours before serving it in an airtight container.

Calories: 293| Fat: 22.5g | Carbs: 24.8g | Fiber: 3.6g|
Sugars: 14.1g | Protein: 2.3g

150. Frozen Fruity Dessert

Total Prep Time: 10 Minutes| Total Cook Time: 20 Minutes | Makes: 6 Servings

INGREDIENTS:
14-ounce can of coconut milk
2 tablespoons lime juice
1 cup frozen pineapple chunks, thawed
4 cups frozen banana slices, thawed

DIRECTIONS:
Line a glass casserole dish with plastic wrap.
In a high-powered blender, combine all ingredients and blend until smooth.
Fill the prepared casserole dish equally with the mixture.
Before serving, freeze for about 40 minutes.

Calories: 255| Fat: 16.1g | Carbs: 30.2g | Fiber: 4.4g|
Sugars: 17.2g | Protein: 2.8g

151. Banana and Avocado Pudding

Total Prep Time: 15 Minutes + Refrigeration Time | Makes: 4 Servings

INGREDIENTS:
2 cups bananas, peeled and chopped
2 ripe avocados, peeled and chopped
1 teaspoon lime zest, finely grated
1 teaspoon lemon zest, finely grated
½ cup fresh lime juice
1/3 cup honey
¼ cup almonds, chopped
½ cup lemon juice

DIRECTIONS:
Mix all ingredients and blend until smooth.
Pour the mousse into 4 serving glasses.
Refrigerate for 2-3 hours before serving.
Garnish with nuts and serve.

Calories: 462| Fat: 20.1g | Carbs: 48.2g | Fiber: 10.2g | Sugars: 30.4g | Protein: 3g

152. Mediterranean Pumpkin Cream

Total Prep Time: 15 Minutes| Total Cook Time: 1 Hour | Makes: 6 Servings

INGREDIENTS:
1 cup canned pumpkin
1 teaspoon ground cinnamon
pinch of salt
2 teaspoons of grated nutmeg
2 eggs
¼ teaspoon ground ginger
1 teaspoon vanilla extract
1 cup coconut milk
8-10 drops of liquid stevia

DIRECTIONS:
Preheat your oven to 350ºF.
Combine the pumpkin and spices in a mixing bowl.
In a separate bowl, beat the eggs thoroughly.
Mix in the other ingredients until fully combined.
Add egg mixture to pumpkin mixture and stir until well blended.
Transfer the mixture to 6 ramekins.
place the mussels in a casserole,
Pour about 2-inches of water around the ramekins.
Bake for at least 1 hour.

Calories: 130| Fat: 11.1g | Carbs: 6.1g | Fiber: 2.3g| Sugars: 2.9g | Protein: 3.3g

153. Citrusy Strawberry Soufflé

Total Prep Time: 15 Minutes| Total Cook Time: 12 Minutes | Makes: 6 Servings

INGREDIENTS:
18 ounces fresh strawberries, peeled
1/3 cup raw honey
5 egg whites
4 teaspoons fresh lemon juice

DIRECTIONS:
Preheat your oven to 350ºF.
Place the strawberries in a blender and blend until it reaches a puree form. Pass the seeds through a sieve.
In a bowl, combine the strawberry purée, 3 tablespoons of honey, 2 proteins, and the lemon juice, and pulse until fluffy and light. In another bowl, add the remaining proteins and beat until fluffy. Gradually beating, add the remaining honey, and beat until stiff peaks form.
Gently stir the Proteins into the strawberry mixture.
Transfer the mixture evenly into 6 large ramekins. Arrange the molds on a baking sheet. Cook for about 10-12 minutes.
Remove from oven and serve immediately.

Calories: 100| Fat: 0.3g | Carbs: 22.3g | Fiber: 1.8g| Sugars: 19.9g | Protein: 3.7g

154. Very Spicy Pumpkin Pie

Total Prep Time: 15 Minutes| Total Cook Time: 1 Hour 15 Minutes | Makes: 8 Servings

INGREDIENTS:
FOR THE CRUST:
2 tablespoons coconut oil
2½ cups almonds
1 teaspoon baking powder
1 teaspoon of salt
FOR FILLING:
1 can (15 ounces) of unsweetened pumpkin puree
1 tablespoon arrowroot powder
½ teaspoon ground nutmeg
½ teaspoon ground cinnamon
¼ teaspoon ground ginger
¼ teaspoon ground cardamom
¼ teaspoon ground cloves
pinch of salt
1 cup coconut milk
3 eggs, beaten
3 tablespoons raw honey

DIRECTIONS:
Preheat your oven to 350ºF.
For the crust, add the nuts, baking soda, coconut oil, and salt to a processor and pulse.
Place crust mixture in a 9-inch cake pan.
Place the cake tin on a baking sheet.
Bake for about 15 minutes.
Meanwhile, put all the filling ingredients in a bowl and mix well.
Remove the crust from the oven.
Spoon the mixture into the crust.
Bake for about 50 minutes.
Freeze about 3-4 hours before serving.

Calories: 411| Fat: 35.5g | Carbs: 17.8g | Fiber: 5g| Sugars: 9.8g | Protein: 12.8g

155. Mediterranean Zucchini Brownies

Total Prep Time: 15 Minutes| Total Cook Time: 45 Minutes | Makes: 20 Sliced

INGREDIENTS:
1½ cups zucchini, grated
1 cup dark chocolate chips
1/3 cup honey
1 egg
1 cup almond butter
1 teaspoon baking powder
1 teaspoon ground cinnamon
½ teaspoon ground nutmeg
1 teaspoon vanilla extract

DIRECTIONS:
Mix all of the ingredients and stir thoroughly.
Pour the mixture into the prepared pan evenly.
Bake for about 35 minutes at 350°F.
Remove from the oven and let cool completely.
Cut into desired squares and serve.

Calories: 56| Fat: 2.3g | Carbohydrates: 9.3g| Fiber: 0.3g|
Sugars: 8.1g | Protein: 1g

156. Almond Cake in a Mug

Total Prep Time: 10 Minutes| Total Cook Time: 2 Minutes | Makes: 1 Serving

INGREDIENTS:
3 tablespoons of almond flour
1 banana, mashed
½ teaspoon baking powder
1 tablespoon coconut blossom
sugar
½ teaspoon ground cinnamon
Pinch of ground ginger
Pinch of salt
1 tablespoon coconut oil,
softened
½ teaspoon vanilla extract

DIRECTIONS:
In a mixing dish, combine all of the ingredients and stir
thoroughly.
Transfer the mixture to a microwave-safe mug.
Microwave on high power for about 2 minutes.

Calories: 382| Fat: 22.9g | Carbs: 45.3g | Fiber: 6g | Sugars:
27.5g | Protein: 5.1g

157. Pineapple Cake

Total Prep Time: 15 Minutes| Total Cook Time: 50 Minutes | Makes: 6 Servings

INGREDIENTS:
5 tablespoons raw honey
2 slices of fresh pineapple
15 fresh sweet cherries
1 cup almond flour
½ teaspoon baking powder
2 eggs
3 tablespoons coconut oil, melted
1 teaspoon vanilla extract

DIRECTIONS:
Preheat your oven to 350°F.
In an 8-inch round cake pan, evenly spread about 1½ tablespoons of honey.
Arrange the pineapple slices and 15 cherries on top of the honey.
Bake for about 15 minutes.
Combine almond flour and baking powder in a bowl.
In another bowl, add the eggs and the rest of the honey and beat until creamy.
Beat in the coconut oil and vanilla essence.
Mix in the flour, baking powder, and salt.
Spread the flour mixture evenly over the pineapple and cherries.
Bake for 35 minutes.
Invert the cooled cake onto a serving dish.

Calories: 258| Fat: 17.1g | Carbs: 21.6g | Fiber: 2.4g| Sugars: 16.8 g | Protein: 6.1g

158. Unbaked Brownie Balls

Total Prep Time: 10 Minutes| Makes: 4 Servings

INGREDIENTS:
1 1/2 cups walnuts
Pinch of low sodium salt
a few drops of stevia
1 teaspoon vanilla
1/3 cup unsweetened cocoa powder

DIRECTIONS:
In a food processor, combine walnuts and salt.
In a blender, combine the vanilla, cocoa powder, and stevia.
Now mix all of the ingredients.
While the blender is still running, drizzle in a few drops of water at a time to bind the mixture together.
Transfer the mixture to a bowl with a spatula. Form small round balls with your hands, rolling them in your palms.
Refrigerate it for a few hours.

Calories: 328|Fat: 4.5 g|Saturated Fat: 0.9 g|Cholesterol: 0 mg|Protein: 6.6 g|Carbohydrates: 73.6 g|Sugar: 47.2 g|Fiber: 9.6 g|Sodium: 85 mg|Calcium: 56 mg|Iron: 2.7 mg

159. Mediterranean Pumpkin Cake

Total Prep Time: 10 Minutes| Total Cook Time: 20 Minutes | Makes: 4 Servings

INGREDIENTS:
1 cup pumpkin puree
2 cups blanched almond flour
2 teaspoons ground cinnamon
a few drops of stevia
½ cup flaxseed meal
1 tablespoon vanilla extract
½ teaspoon low sodium salt
1 egg

DIRECTIONS:
Combine the almond flour, flaxseed meal, cinnamon, and low sodium salt in a mixing bowl.
Combine the egg, pumpkin, and vanilla extract with the help of a spatula.
To make a batter, gently combine the dry and wet components, being careful not to overmix or the batter will become greasy and dense.
Spoon the batter into a pan lined with parchment paper.
Bake at 350°F for 20 minutes.

Calories: 125|Fat: 0.5|Carbohydrates: 25|Fiber: 1|Protein: 4.5

160. Chocolatey Spinach Brownies

Total Prep Time: 14 Minutes| Total Cook Time: 40 Minutes | Makes: 6 Servings

INGREDIENTS:
½ cup extra virgin coconut oil
4 drops of stevia
1 ¼ cup frozen chopped spinach
6 oz. sugar-free chocolate
½ cup coconut oil
6 eggs
pinch cinnamon
½ teaspoon cream of tartar
½ cup cocoa powder
1 teaspoon vanilla pod
¼ teaspoon baking soda
½ teaspoon low sodium salt

DIRECTIONS:
Preheat the oven to 325 degrees Fahrenheit.
Melt the coconut oil and chocolate together in the microwave. Toss in the vanilla extract and whisk to combine. Allow cooling. Combine the cocoa powder, baking soda, cream of tartar, low-sodium salt, and cinnamon in a mixing bowl. In a food processor or blender, combine spinach and egg until fully smooth. In a food processor, combine the coconut oil and pulse until smooth. Slowly pour the melted chocolate mixture into the egg mixture, along with 4 drops of stevia liquid, and blend.
Mix in the dry ingredients until completely combined.
Spread the batter evenly in the prepared baking pan with a spatula. Bake for 40 minutes.

Calories 114.3|Total Fat 8.2 g|Saturated Fat 2.8 g|Polyunsaturated Fat 2.9 g|Monounsaturated Fat 2.2 g|Cholesterol 26.0 mg|Sodium 276.7 mg|Potassium 82.7 mg|Total Carbohydrate 5.3 g|Dietary Fiber 1.0 g|Sugars 0.1 g|Protein 4.0 g

161. Chestnut-Cacao-Almond Cake

Total Prep Time: 10 Minutes| Total Cook Time: 35 Minutes | Makes: 4 Servings

INGREDIENTS:
1/2 teaspoon cream of tartar
1/2 cup raw cacao powder
1 cup chestnut flour
Handful crushed chestnuts
4 drops of stevia
1/2 teaspoon baking soda
1/2 cup ground almonds
3 eggs, separated
3/4 cup coconut milk

DIRECTIONS:
Preheat the oven to 350°F.
Whisk the egg whites and cream of tartar.
Combine the egg yolks, chestnut flour, ground almonds, stevia, raw cacao, baking soda, and coconut milk in a separate mixing dish.
Fold in the egg whites and blend until no visible white remains.
Pour the mixture into the pie/tart pan.
If desired, top with crushed chestnuts.
Bake on the center rack for 35 minutes.

Calories: 201 |37g Fat |23g Saturated Fat |69g Carbs |39g Sugar |8.9g Protein |2.6g Fiber |0.29g Sodium

CONCLUSION

The Mediterranean diet is full of Fruits, vegetables, fish, olive oil, whole grains, legumes, and nuts and each of these components, according to experts, is healthful and provides good nutrients and general wellness.

The Mediterranean diet has also been demonstrated to be good to the gut. This diet's high fiber content can help keep bowel motions regular and smooth. The diet also contributes to the growth of beneficial gut flora, which aids in a variety of physiological processes, including immunity and overall health.

This diet's anti-oxidant and anti-inflammatory components can also help to slow down the aging process and promote brain function. Consumers, particularly postmenopausal women, benefit from the calcium-rich components of this diet, which improve bone and muscle health. Diabetes, dyslipidemia (high cholesterol), memory loss and dementia, breast cancer, depression, and other disorders are all prevented by eating a healthy diet. According to specialists, it also aids in maintaining a healthy body weight.

And the best thing is that unlike most other diets, the Mediterranean diet is simple to follow and to stick to!

Happy cooking from this book!

INDEX

Southwestern pork stew; 39
Spicy sweet potato breakfast bowl; 22
Spicy turkey stir fry; 49
Spinach, shrimp & tangerine bowl; 73
Split peas with spinach; 68
Squash and lentil soup; 75
Stir-fried vegetables & rice; 67
Stuffed pork tenderloin & radish; 47
Sumac cod in tomato sauce; 63
Sunflower seed pesto chicken; 51
Sweet potato chicken dumplings; 53

T

Taco lettuce cups; 51
Tater tot nachos; 44
Tofu and capers pizza; 84
Tomato & cauliflower spaghetti; 80

Tortellini salad with spinach; 78
Tortilla chips; 88
Turkey squash scramble; 49
Turkey stuffed boats; 50
Turmeric roasted cauliflower; 35

U

Unbaked brownie balls; 96

V

Vegetable mediterranean pasta; 80
Veggie-stuffed tomatoes; 72
Velveeta and ground beef dinner; 40
Very spicy pumpkin pie; 94

W

Walnut and almond porridge; 25

Made in United States
North Haven, CT
15 July 2022

21412757R00057